SWIFT LEADERSHIP

EXPLORING EFFECTIVE LEADERSHIP PRACTICES THROUGH POPULAR CULTURE

Series editor: Michael J. Urick

The aim of this series is to examine modern and innovative business theories and methods via relatable popular cultural themes. The books will provide academically rigorous and credible applications and solutions to practitioners and upper-level business students, in a format designed to be highly engaging and effective.

Titles in Exploring Effective Leadership Practices Through Popular Culture

A Manager's Guide to Using the Force: Leadership Lessons from a Galaxy Far Far Away
Michael J. Urick
Leadership in Middle Earth: Theories and Applications for Organizations
Michael J. Urick
Leadership Insights for Wizards and Witches
Aditya Simha
Leaders Assemble! Leadership in the MCU
Gordon B. Schmidt and Sy Islam
Bend the Knee or Seize the Throne: Leadership Lessons from Westeros
Nathan Tong and Michael J. Urick
Courageous Companions: Followership in Doctor Who
Kimberly Yost
Against All Odds: Leadership and the Handmaid's Tale
Cristina de Mello-e-Souza Wildermuth
Elements of Leadership: Lessons from Avatar the Last Airbender
Sy Islam and Gordon B. Schmidt
Leadership Lessons from the Kardashians: Bodies, Emotions, Success
Brigitte Biehl

Forthcoming

Leaders of the Caribbean
Pelin Kohn and Michael J. Urick
Slaying the Vampires, Werewolves and Demons of Ineffective Leadership
Aditya Simha

SWIFT LEADERSHIP

A Taylor-made Approach to Influence and Decision Making

By

Mariah Yates
Western Kentucky University, USA

And

Michael J. Urick
Saint Vincent College, USA

emerald
PUBLISHING

United Kingdom – North America – Japan
India – Malaysia – China

Emerald Publishing Limited

Emerald Publishing, Floor 5, Northspring, 21-23 Wellington Street, Leeds LS1 4DL.

First edition 2025

Reprints and permissions service
Contact: www.copyright.com

British Library Cataloguing in Publication Data
A catalogue record for this book is available from the British Library

ISBN: 978-1-83549-623-7 (Print)
ISBN: 978-1-83549-620-6 (Online)
ISBN: 978-1-83549-622-0 (Epub)

I would like to dedicate this book to my husband, Adam, and our son, Silas. I love you both dearly. Thank you for your unwavering support and for joining me on this adventure. I also appreciate your tolerance of the constant Taylor Swift music playing throughout our home. – **Mariah Yates**

This book is dedicated to the students of the Alex G. McKenna School of Business, Economics, and Government at Saint Vincent College. You constantly inspire me to be the best I can be. Many of you expressed excitement (and provided ideas) when I talked with you about the possibility of this book. Thank you for your enthusiasm – you make my job worthwhile. – **Michael J. Urick**

CONTENTS

About the Authors   xi

Acknowledgments   xv

1.   ...Ready for It?   1
      Introduction   1
      Overview of the Book   3
      Why Focus on Taylor Swift   5
      Conclusion   7

2.   Wildest Dreams   11
      Visionary Leadership   12
          Goal-setting Theory   12
      Vision of Nashville   13
      Task Behaviors and Task Performance   14
      Conclusion   15

3.   Fearless   17
      Transformational Leadership   18
          Inspirational Motivation   19
          Idealized Influence   20
          Intellectual Stimulation   21
          Individualized Consideration   22
      Conclusion   23

4.   Sparks Fly   27
      Creativity and Innovation   28
      Leadership Styles and Behaviors   29
          Authentic Leadership Style   30
          Entrepreneurial Leadership   32
      Conclusion   33

5. Enchanted   37
    What is Power?   38
        Coercive Power   38
        Reward Power   39
        Legitimate Power   41
        Expert Power   42
        Referent Power   43
    Conclusion   45

6. Speak Now   49
    Leader–Member Exchange Theory   50
    Servant Leadership   53
    Conclusion   56

7. The Story of Us   59
    Social Capital Theory   60
    Hackman's Five Factors of Team Effectiveness   64
    Conclusion   66

8. Out of the Woods   71
    The Five Phases of Crisis Management   72
        Phase 1: Signal Detection   73
        Phase 2: Preparation/Prevention   74
        Phase 3: Damage Containment   74
        Phase 4: Recovery   74
        Phase 5: Learning   75
    Positive Psychological Capital   77
        Hope   77
        Efficacy (Self-efficacy)   78
        Resilience   78
        Optimism   79
    Conclusion   80

9. Anti-hero   85
    Hero Worship   86
        Potential Dangers of Hero Worship   86
        Problems from Emulating Celebrities   87
    Potential Missteps in Swift's Leadership   88
    Conclusion   90

10. All Too Well   93
       Define Your Vision and Set Your Goals   94
       Embodying Transformational Leadership   95
       Tap into Creativity and Innovation   97
       Foster Positive Psychological Capital and Learn How to Turn
       Crisis into Opportunity   98
       Be an Ethical and Authentic Leader   99
       Manage a Successful Team as a Servant Leader   100
       Learn How to Effectively Communicate and Positively
       Influence Others   101
       Be Adaptable   102
       Learn from Failure   102
       Appreciate and Respect Diversity   103
       Conclusion   104

Index   107

ABOUT THE AUTHORS

Mariah Yates is the Director of the Advancing Workplace Culture Initiative at the Gordon Ford College of Business, Western Kentucky University (WKU), where she also serves as an Associate Professor of Management. She earned her PhD in Business Administration with a focus on Organizational Behavior from the University of Cincinnati. Her MBA, with an emphasis on Sustainability, is from Western Kentucky University.

She has developed and taught various undergraduate and graduate courses related to organizational behavior, business ethics, critical thinking in management, and business communication fundamentals. Her research, which primarily explores corporate social responsibility (CSR), organizational behavior, and sustainability, has been widely published in academic journals and has earned her several prestigious awards, including the Matthew Sonfield Research Award from the Small Business Institute and the Best Paper Award from the Academy of Business Research.

Since taking on the role of Director of the Advancing Workplace Culture Initiative, she has been dedicated to promoting an inclusive and equitable workplace culture within the business school. Her leadership has been pivotal in fostering a supportive environment for both faculty and students, aligning with her broader and more recent research interests in diversity, equity, and inclusion.

She is the recipient of numerous accolades for her innovations in teaching and service. These include the Vitale Award for Initiative, Innovation, and Leadership, a National Best Practices Award from the Small Business Institute, and multiple teaching honors from the Center for Innovative Teaching & Learning (CITL) at WKU. She has also helped secure significant grants, such as the Gates Foundation Grant for the AASCU Student Success Equity Intensive.

Her professional affiliations are extensive, including memberships in the Academy of Management, the International Leadership Association, and the Society for Industrial and Organizational Psychology. She serves on the editorial boards of the *Global Journal of Management and Marketing* and *the Journal of Small Business Strategy* and is a frequent reviewer for several other academic journals.

In addition to her academic roles, she actively contributes to her community. She is a Board Member of Phoenix Rising Inc., a nonprofit organization focused on combating human trafficking, and has organized various community awareness and fundraising events.

Her professional background also included co-owning and managing Quality Security & Surveillance LLC, providing her with practical business experience that complemented her academic expertise. This unique blend of practical and academic experience positions her as a distinguished figure in the fields of management and organizational behavior.

In her spare time, she enjoys gardening, embroidery work, and traveling with her family and friends.

Michael J. Urick is Dean of the Alex G. McKenna School of Business, Economics, and Government at Saint Vincent College in Latrobe, Pennsylvania (USA) as well as a Professor of Management and Operational Excellence.

He received his PhD in Management (Organizational Behavior focus) from the University of Cincinnati. His MBA (focused in Human Resources Management) and MS (in Leadership and Business Ethics) are both from Duquesne University in Pittsburgh and his Bachelor's degree in Accounting with Management and English minors is from Saint Vincent College. He has taught undergraduate and graduate courses related to organizational behavior, human resources, communication, conflict, organizational culture, operations, and research methods. His research has been widely cited in academic publications as well as in news media outlets such as *the Wall Street Journal* and *the BBC*.

The Master of Science in Management: Operational Excellence program at Saint Vincent, which he directed for nearly 10 years prior to his role as Dean, focuses on providing aspiring leaders with cutting edge management techniques to effectively problem solve, minimize waste, and continuously improve their organizations. Under his directorship, the program was consistently ranked as a "Top 50 Best Value Master's in Management" program by Value Colleges and as a "Top Online Non-MBA Business Graduate Degree" by US News and World Report.

He is Six Sigma Green Belt Certified, Diversity Management Certified, a Certified Conflict Manager, Project Management Essentials Certified, and MBTI Certified and is also certified through the Society for Human Resource Management as well as the True Lean program at the University of Kentucky. He is the Recipient of an "Excellence in Teaching" award from the Lindner College of Business at the University of Cincinnati, the "Quentin Schaut Faculty Award" from Saint Vincent College, and a "Teaching Excellence" award from the Accreditation Council for Business Schools and Programs among other pedagogical honors. Internationally, he was also recognized by the Institute for Supply Management as a "Person of the Year" in the learning and education category.

He is an Associate Editor of *the Journal of Leadership and Management* based in Poland, the North American Associate Editor of *the Measuring Business Excellence journal*, and on the editorial board of *Management Teaching Review*. He is also the Editor for the *"Exploring Effective Leadership Practices through Popular Culture"* book series from Emerald Publishing.

His research interests include leadership, conflict, and identity in the workplace. Much of his work focuses on issues related to intergenerational phenomena within organizations. He also often examines how popular culture can be used to advance organizational behavior theory. In addition to authoring or coauthoring over 50 publications including multiple books and peer-reviewed articles, he has regularly presented at academic and practitioner international meetings such as the Academy of Management, Society for Industrial and Organizational Psychology, and Institute for Supply Management conferences. He is a regular speaker on age-related issues in the workplace throughout the USA and internationally (having presented on four continents including presentations at the University of Oxford in the UK) and served as a consultant on issues related to workplace interactions, organizational culture, and ethics for various organizations. He has served as a Reviewer for a variety of academic publications including the *Journal of Intergenerational Relationships*, *Journal of Social Psychology*, *Journal of Organizational Behavior*, and *Journal of Family Issues* as well as *the Organizational Behavior and Human Resources* divisions of the Academy of Management Annual Meeting in addition to other conferences.

Professionally, he has served on the boards of ISM-Pittsburgh (in various roles including President) and the Westmoreland Arts and Heritage Festival (a top-rated community event). He has also served on the Westmoreland

Human Resources Association (a regional SHRM chapter) board in various positions including Vice President. Prior to academia, he worked in a variety of roles related to auditing, utilities, environmental issues, and training and development. Through these experiences, he became fascinated with interactions in the workplace and how they might be improved which has influenced his academic career.

For fun, he enjoys music and, since 1998, has been a semiprofessional jazz musician and toured through over a dozen US states while releasing multiple recordings with various ensembles.

ACKNOWLEDGMENTS

First and foremost, I want to express my deepest gratitude to my husband, Adam, and our son, Silas. Your all's willingness to be flexible in allowing me to lock myself away in the office to write, coupled with your continuous support and encouragement, are what made this book possible.

I extend my profound thanks to my coauthor, Mike Urick, for inviting me to join this exciting project and giving me the opportunity to write my first book. Your guidance and partnership have been invaluable.

To the amazing team at Emerald – Fiona Allison, Lydia Cutmore, Joshi Monica Jerome, Yemaya Marsden, and Sangeetha Rajan – thank you for your assistance and for believing in me as a writer. Your support has been instrumental in bringing this book to life.

I am also deeply grateful to Taylor Swift for inspiring me and so many others to embrace our own authentic forms of leadership. Your journey has provided a rich source of insights and motivation.

To my fellow Swifties, thank you for your extensive research materials and for being one of the most welcoming and encouraging fandoms out there. Your passion and dedication have enriched this project in countless ways.

Lastly, I want to thank you, the reader, for picking up this book. Your interest and engagement are what make this work meaningful. I hope you find inspiration and valuable insights within these pages.

– Mariah Yates

There are many people that I would like to thank, without whom this book would not be possible.

First, I would like to thank Janet and Lucy. Thank you for putting up with my crazy schedule, multitasking, and taking on too many projects than I can actually handle. Thank you also for understanding my more frequent listening to Taylor Swift while coauthoring this book than I had in the past.

Thank you to my parents, Richard and Michele. Along with my grandfather, Michael "Ug" Cilli, you fostered in me a love of music and writing from a very young age.

Thank you to lead author Mariah Yates. I appreciate our working together and your dedication to seeing this project through.

We could not have completed this book without the assistance of Fiona Allison, Lydia Cutmore, Hemavathi Rajendran, Aimee Wright, Madison Klopfer, Joshi Monica Jerome, Sangeetha Rajan, and all the crew at Emerald. You are all amazing. Thank you for all that you did to get this book published and all that you do for the success of the book series.

Thank you to my students, to whom this book is dedicated, for keeping me young and for making my day job as dean worthwhile.

I'd like to thank my assistant, Lana Dillon, for helping me to find free time in my hectic schedule to devote to fun projects like this.

Thank you to Mark Kachmar for challenging my belief that Taylor Swift is a skilled leader. Because of our conversations, you have made my beliefs that Taylor Swift is a leader worthy of study stronger and, in turn, my arguments for studying leadership through her more pronounced.

Of course, this book would not be possible without Taylor Swift and the team that allows her to write and perform music. Thank you for providing the soundtrack of a generation and for giving us a book's worth of thoughts to consider when exploring leadership.

I also thank God for blessing me with the joy of and ability to write this book and to enjoy both music and studying leadership.

Lastly, thank you, the reader, for picking up a copy of this book. I hope you find it both useful and interesting.

– Michael J. Urick

1

...READY FOR IT?[1]

ABSTRACT

This chapter is an introduction to the book "Swift Leadership: A Taylor-made Approach to Influence and Decision Making" *which is part of the* "Exploring Effective Leadership Practices Through Popular Culture" *series. The book explores the business practices, decisions, and influence tactics used by popular musician and icon Taylor Swift. Swift leverages her popularity to stand up to entertainment industry giants and champion the underdog. This first chapter provides an overview of the book and reasons why analyzing Swift's leadership approach is helpful.*

Keywords: Influence tactics; decisions; introduction; popular culture; Taylor Swift leadership

INTRODUCTION

Taylor Swift was born in December 1989 in a small town in Pennsylvania (USA), and over the next 35 years, would rise to arguably become one of the most popular and influential performers of all time. But this book is not a biography of Swift; rather, it is an examination of what has made her successful as a leader.

---

[1]Swift, T. (2017). ...Ready for It? [Song]. On *Reputation*. Big Machine Records.

When discussing about writing this book with a colleague, one of its authors was confronted with the statement that Taylor Swift was not truly a leader. After all, she (at the time of writing this book) was not an elected official, did not hold an executive position in a Fortune 500 organization, nor commanded a large organization from the top of its hierarchy. However, our view is that Swift is a leader nonetheless.

While we conclude this chapter with a few reasons why it makes sense to think about leadership, using examples from Swift's life and her songs, it suffices to say that we believe her to be a leader based on our working definition of "leadership." We believe that leadership is an activity in which a person influences others while resisting unwanted influence in return (Daft, 2014). Furthermore, leadership requires an individual to make decisions (Vroom & Yetton, 1973).

Swift is both an influencer and decision-maker and, therefore, a leader. She influences millions of fans worldwide as a role model, influencing them to purchase her music and shell out sizable amounts of money to attend her concerts. She makes many decisions as she is the CEO of her brand. It should be noted that many of these decisions benefit others, even just by bringing personal enjoyment from her music. In contrast, some of her decisions have sent significant shockwaves through the industries she is a part of – more on how her decisions have made an impact later.

An astute reader may ask, what is the purpose of exploring Taylor Swift and her leadership? Our purpose is consistent with other books in this "Exploring Effective Leadership Practices through Popular Culture" series. Using fun and engaging examples of popular culture (such as Taylor Swift) can clarify leadership ideas and theories for readers (Urick, 2021). Readers will be presented with academically supported leadership theories, concepts, and techniques, followed by examples from Swift's own leadership approach to make them clearer. We hope readers will then learn these theories, concepts, and techniques to reflect on their leadership style and see how they might be adopted.

That is not to say that readers should do exactly what Taylor Swift does. That would be a mistake because every leader's context is unique and different in some way (Oc, 2018). Very few of us will be international multimedia superstars in the same way that Swift is. So, it does not make sense to do EXACTLY what Swift does. Instead, we should look at what worked for Swift, understand the theory behind why it worked (or did not work) for her, and then determine if there is a way we can leverage that understanding to adapt it to fit our context.

This chapter is an introduction to the book. We hope to make leadership concepts clearer to readers by illustrating them through examples from Taylor Swift. This chapter will now present an overview of what readers might expect from this book, followed by our elaboration on why we think focusing on Swift to learn about leadership is useful.

OVERVIEW OF THE BOOK

Before getting too far ahead with describing why we think examining Taylor Swift's leadership is valid, it may first be interesting to the reader to get a sense of what this book will cover. This section provides a preview of each of the upcoming chapters, named for some of Swift's songs that are most relevant to the chapter's topic.

The first chapter, titled "…Ready for It?," provides a brief overview of the book. We suggest why examining Swift's approach to leadership is useful by highlighting many of her records and suggesting how she fought against some major music industry institutions. Swift often champions the underdog and, in doing so, exerts influence and makes decisions, which are two hallmarks of leaders, thus making her a valuable and exciting example to consider.

In the second chapter of "Wildest Dreams,[2]" we consider the concept of visionary leadership, in which a goal can be a driving, influential force. We consider goal-setting theory and explore how it relates to Swift's early career dream of recording in Nashville. We then discuss the importance of pursuing a vision once it is set and consider that it should align with the knowledge, skills, and abilities of oneself or those that a leader hopes to influence.

The third chapter, "Fearless,[3]" explores transformational leadership and suggests that Swift engages in inspirational motivation, idealized influence, intellectual stimulation, and individualized consideration. Many specific examples from Swift's career will illustrate these "Four I's" of transformational leadership.

---

[2]Swift, T. (2021). Wildest Dreams [Song]. *On Wildest Dreams* (Taylor's Version). Republic Records.

[3]Swift, T. (2021). Fearless [Song]. *On Fearless* (Taylor's Version). Republic Records.

"Sparks Fly"[4] is the fourth chapter of the book. In this chapter, we define creativity and innovation and suggest how they can be drivers for success. We then consider how different leadership styles relate to creativity and innovation and suggest that, through authentic leadership, Swift has become influential and inspired creativity among her followers. Likewise, by taking an entrepreneurial approach to leadership, Swift was able to take more charge of her career and trajectory as an artist, thereby maximizing her creativity.

The fifth chapter, "Enchanted,[5]" considers how leaders become influential by possessing power. This chapter considers the five classic bases of power: legitimate, reward, coercive, expert, and referent. We provide clear evidence of how Taylor Swift leveraged each of the bases to become an influential leader.

"Speak Now,"[6] the sixth chapter of the book, describes Swift's ability to leverage her influence to make important decisions and to advocate for what she cares about. This chapter considers Leader–Member Exchange (LMX) Theory and suggests that Swift is influential with her in-group (her super fans often known as Swifties). But she also impacts other groups, including those who are only casual fans who are familiar with Swift's biggest hits and even individuals who dislike the singer and are decidedly anti-Swift. This chapter also explores Servant Leadership and provides examples of how Swift uses her influence to impact broad social issues (Greenleaf, 1977).

In "The Story of Us,"[7] the book's seventh chapter, we consider teams. Swift has done a considerable job of putting together a group of people to provide advice, support, resources, and essential functions for her product. We examine how she did this by considering social capital theory and explaining Swift's approach to building and leveraging professional relationships. We then consider what makes groups effective and suggest that Swift surrounds herself with people who exhibit team characteristics, are guided by a compelling direction, are enabled by a clear structure, are supported and supportive, and experience coaching.

The eighth chapter considers crisis and unpredictability. Its title is "Out of the Woods,"[8] which reflects some of the crises that Swift faced and how

---

[4]Swift, T. (2023). Sparks Fly [Song]. *On Speak Now* (Taylor's Version). Republic Records.
[5]Swift, T. (2023). Enchanted [Song]. *On Speak Now* (Taylor's Version). Republic Records.
[6]Swift, T. (2023). Speak Now [Song]. *On Speak Now* (Taylor's Version). Republic Records.
[7]Swift, T. (2023). The Story of Us [Song]. *On Speak Now* (Taylor's Version). Republic Records.
[8]Swift, T. (2021). Out of the Woods [Song]. *On 1989* (Taylor's Version). Republic Records.

she responded to them, including her decision to re-record her entire music catalog when faced with losing ownership of her albums. In this chapter, we explore the five phases of crisis management and provide examples of Swift progressing through these stages. We also suggest the importance of maintaining a positive psychological mindset while facing crisis situations by providing examples from Swift's career. In doing so, we consider the importance of hope, self-efficacy, resilience, and optimism.

"Anti-Hero"[9] is the ninth chapter and is a bit more critical of Swift's leadership than prior chapters. It considers some of the pitfalls of idolizing leaders (and celebrities) such as Taylor Swift. Furthermore, it suggests that each leader's context is unique, and thus, it is crucial to consider one's unique situation when trying to emulate the behaviors of other role model leaders. Furthermore, it presents a critique of some potential missteps of Swift's approach to influence and decision-making, including her use of a private jet, involvement with politics, and responsibility as a role model to consider the content of her art.

"All Too Well"[10] is the concluding chapter of the book. In it, we summarize all of the content covered thus far and make suggestions for important takeaways that we hope readers will consider. We also reflect on the leadership lessons that Taylor Swift can teach us.

Throughout the book, we will explore the above in significant detail using examples from Taylor Swift's life and career as appropriate. Hopefully, you now have a sense of the direction of the book and are already starting to believe that Taylor Swift is an appropriate person to consider to learn more about leadership. The following section will further make the case for our rationale in looking at Swift's leadership approach.

WHY FOCUS ON TAYLOR SWIFT

At this point, you may be wondering to yourself: but why Taylor Swift? Aren't there other world leaders to examine who are more impactful to important social phenomena such as global conflict and the economy? Moreover, aren't there other ways to learn about leadership in a fun way other than exploring concepts through the examples of Taylor Swift? Absolutely! However, as we

---

[9]Swift, T. (2022). Anti-Hero [Song]. On *Midnights*. Republic Records.
[10]Swift, T. (2021). All Too Well [Song]. *On Red* (Taylor's Version). Republic Records.

have already stated, leadership concepts can be illustrated effectively through Swift, and in so doing, we aim to reach a broad audience.

Furthermore, in this book, we will explore many examples that make Swift an appropriate figure to explore leadership concepts. This chapter will focus on four specific examples highlighting the appropriateness of studying her leadership.

First is Swift's devotion to her fans. She has a passionate fanbase who speculate on her every next move on social media. Furthermore, her fans are engaged with her every move in significant ways, downloading and streaming every new Swift song released (including exclusive special bonus tracks). They attend concerts sporting Taylor Swift apparel and exchanging bracelets. They do not just show up – they show up in droves. Swift's Eras tour was the highest-grossing tour ever – and her shows also have higher attendance than uber-popular US sporting events such as the Super Bowl (Rosen, 2023). In some cities, crowds at her Eras Tour shows were so large that they caused earthquakes while dancing in the arena to Swift's tunes (Sykes & Rosenbloom, 2023). Her influence was so impactful that some towns gave her the key to the city, named streets in her honor, and (in the case of Glendale, Arizona) renamed their city in honor of Swift (Masley, 2023).

Second, Swift is more than just the biggest ticket for live music. She is the top-selling artist in the world as of writing this in 2024, and she has been in the number one Billboard spot for some time (Billboard, 2024). She is the only solo artist to have five albums, spend at least six weeks at number one on the Billboard charts – and has surpassed even the Beatles' record of most weeks in Billboard's Top 200 songs (Caulfield, 2024). In 2023, Swift had the most number-one Billboard albums of any female artist – an incredible feat for someone only in their mid-thirties (France, 2023).

It is not just because of her popularity that we chose to focus on Taylor Swift. Our third reason is that she is also a game-changer in the industries in which she operates. For example, Swift chose to re-record all of her albums when she was being treated unfairly by her previous record label so that its management would not get a further cent of royalties (Bruner, 2023). This action upended how artists interface with record labels and called into question who should be owners of master recordings and how artists should be treated. Furthermore, though her concert tickets are expensive, she (along with her fans) battled entertainment giant TicketMaster to stop overcharging for tickets, eventually leading to multiple lawsuits and a US Senate inquiry (Mayer, 2022).

Fourth, we want to note some of Swift's positive contributions. While no leader is perfect, including Taylor Swift, she has done a lot of good. In addition to being a positive influence for her many fans, she also donates generously. For example, during a recent tour stop in Pittsburgh, USA, Swift donated an unprecedented amount to a local food bank that resulted in providing thousands of meals across the region for those in need (Hall, 2023). Swift also paid more than $55 million in bonuses to her tour truck drivers (which they called life-changing) to show her appreciation (Heller, 2023).

For each of these reasons, we see decision-making and the practice of influencing others as the hallmarks of our working definition of leadership. Of course, more examples will be provided throughout the following pages. However, if these are still insufficient, readers may also refer to the late 2023 CNN report that labeled Swift's year the best any business leader had in recent times due to her commercial success and strong business acumen (Mena, 2023).

CONCLUSION

Leaders can come from anywhere. The examples that inspire solid leadership practices in each of us can be found in various places, even in popular culture. This book will explore leadership through examples from music superstar Taylor Swift. As an introduction, this first chapter explored the following:

- There are many definitions of leadership. The one that we choose to focus on in this book is that leadership is a process of influence and requires decision-making. Taylor Swift is an excellent candidate to use to understand leadership phenomena better because she is both influential and makes decisions that impact many others.

- Though more information will be provided throughout, this chapter provides a roadmap to the reader as we begin to consider leadership concepts that can be illustrated through Swift.

- We also considered in some depth reasons why it makes sense to explore leadership via Swift's examples. These reasons included her devotion to fans, record-breaking album and ticket sales, willingness to take on the established status quo, generosity, and being named a successful business leader by CNN.

We are excited to learn more about leadership through Taylor Swift with you throughout the pages of this book.

Each chapter in the book is named after a Taylor Swift song. The next chapter ("Wildest Dreams") considers pursuing a vision and highlights how Swift's devotion to her vision – even from a young age – contributed to her success.

REFERENCES

Billboard. (2024, January 1). *Billboard Artist 100*. https://www.billboard.com/charts/artist-100/

Bruner, R. (2023, October 27). Here's why Taylor Swift is re-releasing her old albums. *Time*.

Caulfield, K. (2024, February 26). Taylor Swift passes the Beatles for most weeks in Billboard 200's top 10 in last 60 years. *Billboard*. Retrieved June 24, 2024, from https://www.billboard.com/music/chart-beat/taylor-swift-passes-the-beatles-most-weeks-billboard-200-top-10-60-years-1235615209/

Daft, R. L. (2014). *The leadership experience*. Cengage Learning.

Dansereau, F., Graen, G., & Haga, W. J. J. (1975). A vertical dyad linkage approach to leadership within formal organizations: A longitudinal investigation of the role making process. *Organizational Behavior and Human Performance*, 13(1), 46–78.

France, L. R. (2023, July 18). Taylor Swift makes history as female artist with the most No. 1 albums. *CNN*.

Greenleaf, R. (1977). *Servant leadership: A journey into the nature of legitimate power and greatness*. Paulist Press.

Hall, T. (2023, June 16). Taylor Swift makes 'generous' donation to Greater Pittsburgh Community Food Bank. *WPXI*.

Heller, C. (2023, August 3). Taylor Swift's longtime truck driver reacts to "Life-Changing" $100,000 bonuses. *E! News*.

Masley, E. (2023, March 13). Swift City, AZ: Glendale rebrands in honor of Taylor Swift's Eras Tour launch this weekend. *Arizona Republic*.

Mayer, E. (2022, November 18). Taylor Swift breaks silence on Ticketmaster chaos: Read full statement. *Newsweek*.

Mena, B. (2023, December 26). Taylor Swift had the best year for any business leader in recent memory. *CNN*. https://edition.cnn.com/2023/12/26/investing/taylor-swift-businessperson-of-the-year/index.html

Oc, B. (2018). Contextual leadership: A systematic review of how contextual factors shape leadership and its outcomes. *The Leadership Quarterly*, 29(1), 218–235.

Rosen, C. (2023, November 30). Taylor Swift's Eras Tour primed to become highest-grossing ever: Report. *The Messenger*.

Sykes, J., & Rosenbloom, A. (2023, July 28). Taylor Swift fans 'Shake It Off,' causing record-breaking seismic activity during Seattle shows. *CNN*.

Urick, M. J. (2021). *A manager's guide to using the force: Leadership lessons from a galaxy far far away*. Emerald Publishing Limited.

Vroom, V. H., & Yetton, P. W. (1973). *Leadership and decision-making* (Vol. 110). University of Pittsburgh Pre.

2

WILDEST DREAMS[1]

ABSTRACT

This chapter explores the concept of "vision" as it relates to leadership. A vision can be similar to a goal or even, as the Taylor Swift song is titled, part of a leader's "Wildest Dreams." This chapter defines the term "vision" and suggests its relationship to a goal. It provides some characteristics of strong goals as suggested by goal-setting theory (Locke & Latham, 2019). Then, using Taylor Swift as an example leader, it discusses the importance of goal commitment and seeing a vision through to completion.

Keywords: Visionary leadership; vision; goals; goal setting theory; Taylor Swift leadership

"Wildest Dreams" is a popular song from Swift that was initially released in 2014 on her 1989 album. The song recounts a Lover's hope that she will not be forgotten after a breakup. Taking romance out of the equation, Taylor Swift had what some might have called a wild dream before becoming a star. Swift's dream, or vision (a more leadership-friendly term), allowed her to continuously be remembered by millions of fans and by society as a whole. This chapter will explore Swift's vision, including how it helped her find her voice early on in her career and guided her success as her career continued.

---

[1] Swift, T. (2021). Wildest Dreams [Song]. *On Wildest Dreams* (Taylor's Version). Republic Records.

VISIONARY LEADERSHIP

In his famous work, "Visionary Leadership," Burt Nanus (1995) discusses the importance of having a vision. According to Nanus and others who advocate for visionary leadership, it is the responsibility of a leader to articulate and pursue a vision. From this standpoint, a vision can be seen as a goal or a dream.

Goal-setting Theory

In many ways, a vision is like a long-term goal, defined as an objective, an aspiration, or even (like Swift's song) a dream (Merriam-Webster, n.d.). According to goal-setting theory, a goal is most useful if it can increase performance and meets several characteristics (Locke & Latham, 2019). Fig. 1 summarizes four such characteristics.

Fig. 1.   Goal Setting Theory.

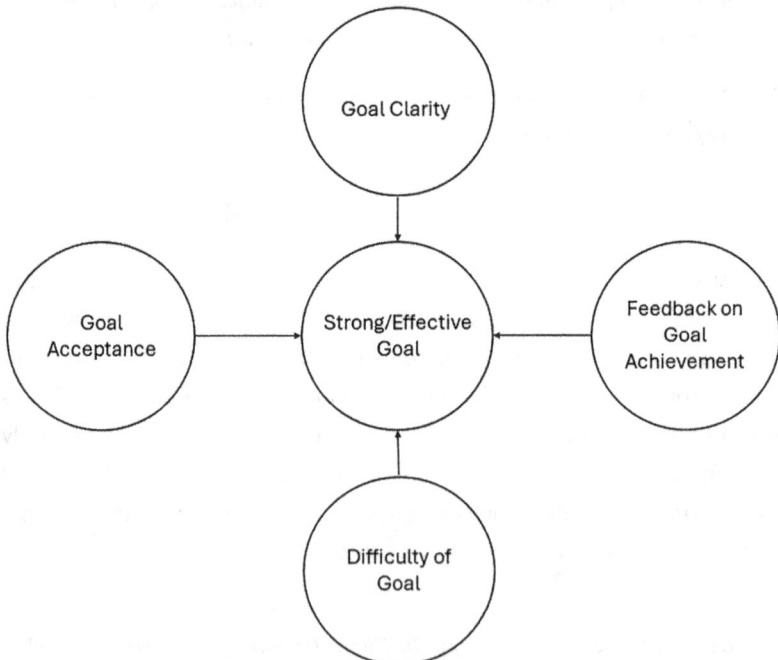

Source: Adapted from Locke and Latham (2019).

The first characteristic of a good goal is that it is clear. In order to drive performance, a goal must be articulated and easily understood. It must be grasped by those who are expected to achieve it.

The second characteristic is that goal attainment must be measured by feedback. The person seeking to achieve the goal must know how well they are progressing toward the vision. This way, they will know how much longer and harder they need to work.

The third characteristic is that the goal should be difficult. A goal should be challenging; otherwise, a person or persons will not achieve their true potential performance. The caveat is that a goal should not be impossible, as it becomes discouraging when people cannot achieve it.

The last characteristic considered here is that the goal must be accepted. The person achieving the goal has to believe in it and truly desire to perform to the best of their ability to accomplish their dream. Goal-setting theory is often thought of as explaining how and why followers are motivated to accomplish something. Certainly, Swift motivates many of her fans to go to great lengths to support her and her music. However, an even more straight-forward example of goal-setting theory is related to self-leadership (in which individuals guide themselves toward personal goals; Neck et al., 1999) in the case of Swift. Swift used goals/dreams to drive her performance, as the next section describes her vision of going to Nashville, Tennessee (a notable music-focused city in the USA) to record at an early age.

VISION OF NASHVILLE

Swift's success was undoubtedly helped by the privileged life she lived growing up. Being raised in an affluent family (Swift is the daughter of two successful businesspeople, and the mansion she grew up in was valued in 2023 at $800,000; Dodd, 2023; McDowell, 2023) near Reading, Pennsylvania (USA). When Swift realized that she wanted to pursue recording in Nashville at a young age, her family certainly had the means to relocate to Tennessee (Taylor, 2021). However, even given her resources, Swift would not have been successful in her career if she did not have a goal, vision, or dream to set her direction at a young age.

Her dream possessed the four characteristics of a goal that leads to per-formance noted above. First, Swift's goal was clear. The goal of becoming a Nashville recording artist was easy to understand and set a clear direction for the behaviors that Swift (and her family) had to enact in order to achieve it – such as moving from Pennsylvania to Tennessee.

The second characteristic noted above is that a goal should have clear feedback. Swift could know how well she was doing toward goal attainment based on the number of producers and studios she connected with, the dates scheduled for recording sessions, and, ultimately, the release of her recorded work. Through these metrics, Swift could see how she was progressing toward becoming a recording artist in Nashville.

The third characteristic is that a goal should be difficult but not impossible. Certainly, relocating hundreds of miles away and making connections in the tough-to-break-into-recording industry of Nashville presents challenges that make this task difficult. But, it is not impossible. Therefore, this goal meets the characteristics that lead to increased performance.

Lastly, the goal must be accepted. Swift truly wanted to accomplish the goal and held it deep in her heart. Furthermore, her parents seemed to accept it as she influenced them to help with her relocation and make connections to make her dreams come true. Thus, the goal was important to Swift and accepted by her family members.

Of course, leaders not only work to achieve personal goals but also influence others to achieve group goals. In Swift's example noted above, personal goals were leveraged to achieve performance. Yet, readers should consider how they might consider both their own personal goals and how they might advocate for group goals that can also lead to performance.

TASK BEHAVIORS AND TASK PERFORMANCE

We have been talking a lot about performance in this chapter, but we have yet to define it. Job performance can come in several types (Motowidlo, 2003). One type is citizenship behaviors, which are nice to have but not fundamental to contributing to specific goals. Another is counterproductive behaviors, which are negative in nature and, as such, do not apply to the discussion here. The third and most important type for our discussion are task behaviors. Task behaviors are specific things that individuals do that contribute toward goal accomplishment.

Tasks must be aligned with the overall vision. In order to accomplish a goal, each task must be related to that goal in some way. For Swift, moving to Tennessee, making connections, and scheduling studio time with producers were all related to Swift's goal of becoming a Nashville recording artist.

It also helps that Swift's natural talent aligns with her goals and task performance. Though sometimes dismissed for some of her albums being "poppy," Swift truly is a musical prodigy, including having written several of her successful songs as a young kid (Taylor, 2021). In the case of Swift, she is an expert songwriter and skilled musician. The tasks of writing and performing songs are types of task performance that lend themselves well to becoming a recording artist. Thus, it is essential that one's knowledge, skills, and abilities lend themselves toward a propensity for accomplishing task performance that helps to achieve goal attainment.

Not only were Swift's dreams aligned with her abilities and resources to accomplish them, but she never gave up on her goals. Partly because the goal to move to Nashville to record was so precisely clear and partly because she held this goal deep in her heart, and therefore, pursued it passionately. Walt Disney is quoted as saying, "To succeed, work hard, never give up and above all cherish magnificent obsession" (AZ Quotes, n.d.), but Swift might have easily made such a statement because it does speak to her work ethic. Of course, the way she pursued her goal of being a recording artist early in her career is one example of how hard work helped Swift achieve her goal, but her strong work ethic has lasted throughout her career. From the details of planning out her shows and crafting her image to her rigorous touring and recording schedules that have been hallmarks of her career thus far, it is an understatement that Swift is a hard worker, particularly when pursuing her dreams.

CONCLUSION

Taylor Swift is unarguably a hard worker. It is this hard work that has helped her achieve her dreams both early on as an aspirational Nashville recording artist and throughout her career. This chapter explored several ideas, including:

- Whether you call it a goal, vision, or dream, it is useful for leaders to have aspirations that set a direction for decisions and behaviors.

- If a dream/goal is clear, allows for feedback, is challenging but not impossible, and is accepted, then task performance that contributes toward that aspiration will likely be high.

- The better a person's knowledge, skills, and abilities are aligned toward dream accomplishment, and the more resources an individual has that can assist with achieving a goal, the more likely a vision will be achieved.

It should be mentioned again that the example given in this chapter about Swift's desire to be a recording artist is a personal goal. However, goals do not have to be personal – they can also be directed at a group or organization. Though this example was more personal in nature, the principles noted above should also apply to collective goals as well.

REFERENCES

AZ Quotes. (n.d.) *Walt Disney quotes about hard work*. Retrieved January 27, 2024, from https://www.azquotes.com/author/4000-Walt_Disney/tag/hard-work

Dodd, S. (2023, December 18). All about Taylor Swift's parents, Scott and Andrea Swift. *People*.

Locke, E. A., & Latham, G. P. (2019). The development of goal setting theory: A half-century retrospective. *Motivation Science, 5*(2), 93.

McDowell, E. (2023, May 15). Take a look inside Taylor Swift's childhood home in Pennsylvania, a five-bedroom house worth $800,000. *Business Insider*.

Merriam-Webster. (n.d.). *Dream*. Retrieved January 25, 2024, from https://www.merriam-webster.com/dictionary/goal

Motowidlo, S. J. (2003). Job performance. *Handbook of Psychology: Industrial and Organizational Psychology, 12*(4), 39–53.

Nanus, B. (1995). *Visionary leadership* (Vol. 196). John Wiley & Sons.

Neck, C. P., Neck, H. M., Manz, C. C., & Godwin, J. (1999). "I think I can; I think I can": A self-leadership perspective toward enhancing entrepreneur thought patterns, self-efficacy, and performance. *Journal of Managerial Psychology, 14*(6), 477–501.

Taylor, M. F. (2021). *Taylor Swift: The life, loves and music of a global sensation*. New Haven Publishing Limited.

3

FEARLESS

ABSTRACT

This chapter explores the essence of transformational leadership through Taylor Swift's unique perspective on fearlessness, highlighting the importance of resilience and perseverance. Swift's leadership style exemplifies key principles such as inspirational motivation, idealized influence, intellectual stimulation, and individualized consideration. By inspiring fans with a compelling vision, fostering trust through authenticity, engaging creatively with her audience, and supporting individual growth, Swift demonstrates how transformational leadership can drive remarkable success. This chapter provides valuable insights on how transformational leadership (Downton, 1973) can positively impact any team or organization.

Keywords: Transformational leadership; inspirational motivation; idealized influence; intellectual stimulation; individualized consideration; Taylor Swift leadership

To me, "FEARLESS" is not the absence of fear. It's not being completely unafraid. To me, FEARLESS is having fears. FEARLESS is having doubts. Lots of them. To me, FEARLESS is living in spite of those things that scare you to death ... FEARLESS is getting back up and fighting for what you want over and over again... even though every time you've tried before, you've lost. It's FEARLESS to have faith that someday things will change. – Taylor Swift (Swift, 2021).

In her quote, Taylor Swift captures the essence of true fearlessness, emphasizing that it's not about the absence of fear but the determination to face it head-on. This perspective aligns with the principles of transformational leadership, where leaders inspire and motivate others to exceed their own expectations and achieve remarkable feats. Transformational leaders set high standards, cultivate a sense of purpose, and foster a supportive environment where followers are encouraged to develop and grow.

As we delve into the concept of transformational leadership, we will explore how such leaders, like Taylor Swift, utilize inspirational motivation, idealized influence, intellectual stimulation, and individualized consideration to create lasting, positive change. Through examining Swift's leadership style, we will uncover the powerful impact of leading with resilience, authenticity, and an unwavering commitment to one's vision and goals.

TRANSFORMATIONAL LEADERSHIP

Transformational leadership serves to intrinsically motivate others to do more than originally intended, or even thought was possible (Bass & Riggio, 2006). Challenging expectations are set, and high performance is typically achieved. Simultaneously, these transformational leaders tend to have more committed and satisfied followers by empowering them to attend to their own individual needs and development (Bass & Riggio, 2006). Transformational leadership involves moving followers toward a shared commitment of vision or goals for the organization or group by mentoring, coaching, and aiding in the personal development of followers (Bass & Riggio, 2006). While early studies of transformational leadership found the style particularly powerful in military settings (e.g., Bass, 1985; Boyd, 1988; Curphy, 1991), the accumulation of research has shown transformational leadership to be valuable in every sector and setting (Avolio & Yammarino, 2002).

Whether leading a team, an organization, a fan base, or ideological movement, transformational leaders have the potential to create impactful, positive change for all involved. Transformational leaders are often identified through their display of four key characteristics (Bass, 1985): (1) inspirational motivation, (2) idealized influence, (3) intellectual stimulation, and (4) individualized consideration.

Inspirational Motivation

Inspirational motivation is when a leader is effective in communicating a compelling and motivating vision to their followers. Doing so enables followers to have a strong sense of purpose and motivation to act in ways that will aid in bringing the shared vision to life (Bass, 1999). Purpose and meaning ultimately serve as driving factors for propelling groups forward.

Taylor Swift has served as inspiration to her fans for over two decades and has been regarded as a musical trailblazer for the 21st century (Alexander, 2023). Her songwriting abilities and business acumen have influenced artists and entrepreneurs worldwide. *Billboard*, a top American music and entertainment magazine, described Swift as "an advocate, a style icon, a marketing wiz, a prolific songwriter, a pusher of visual boundaries and a record-breaking road warrior" (Schneider, 2023).

In 2022, Swift was bestowed an honorary doctorate at New York University's (NYU) spring graduation ceremony. She was also the event's keynote speaker, in which she imparted several lessons as inspiration to graduates regarding the future that lies ahead. Swift emphasized the importance of showing genuine enthusiasm and effort, and to *"Never be ashamed of trying. Effortlessness is a myth"* (Dailey, 2022). She stressed that moments of failure or rejection can be as crucial as success, stating *"The times I was told no or wasn't included, wasn't chosen, didn't win, didn't make the cut...looking back, it really feels like those moments were as important, if not more crucial, than the moments I was told 'yes'"* (Dailey, 2022). Swift concluded by encouraging graduates to trust their instincts and learn from all experiences, both good and bad. She emphasized resilience and the ability to recover and grow stronger from challenges, stating *"We are led by our gut instincts, our intuition, our desires and fears, our scars and our dreams"* (Dailey, 2022).

Swift often uses speaking events such as this, and interviews, as opportunities to encourage followers (and people in general) to enthusiastically pursue their own purpose and vision to achieve an enriching life. She is realistic in acknowledging that there will be struggles along the way, but that resilience is a key ingredient in the pursuit of any goal or dream.

Idealized Influence

Idealized influence is displayed when the leader serves as a positive role model for followers by engaging in ethical behaviors, instilling a sense of trust and respect. Role models are depicted as having the ability to inspire other people to engage in novel behaviors and set ambitious goals for themselves (Morgenroth et al., 2015). Role models are often especially impactful when it comes to members of underrepresented and stigmatized groups (Morgenroth et al., 2015). Followers tend to develop positive emotional attachments to the leader when they see behavioral integrity displayed (Bass & Riggio, 2006). This is often demonstrated through a consistency in the leader's espoused values and their subsequent actions, that is, "walking the walk," not just "talking the talk." Transformational leaders who are strong in idealized influence are found to be more consistent in moral and ethical behaviors overall (Okoli et al., 2021). These characteristics make the leaders worthy of followers' admiration and trust (Kitur et al., 2020).

Whether it be figures from history, religion, politics, or popular culture, famous individuals have often been examined in terms of whether they positively model what it means to be a "good person" in the world (Hammond et al., 2022). Swift has often been regarded as a positive role model due to her consistent pursuit of authenticity, that is, "walking the walk" (Bulgarella, 2023). Harter (2002) describes authenticity as owning one's personal experiences, thoughts, beliefs, emotions, and desires. Therefore, authenticity involves being self-aware and acting in accordance with what one genuinely thinks and believes (Luthans & Avolio, 2003). Those that embody idealized influence are often regarded as authentic leaders, as they are "genuine people who are true to themselves and to what they believe in. They engender trust and develop genuine connections with others. Because people trust them, they are able to motivate others to high levels of performance" (George et al., 2007, p. xxxi).

Forbes has recognized Swift's unique ability to tap into authenticity and encourages organizations to do the same to foster positive workplaces (Bulgarella, 2023). Both within and outside of the workplace, people are seeking genuine connection with themselves and others. Organizations can take a page out of Swift's playbook by holding themselves to a high set of ethical standards that employees are happy to align themselves with.

Intellectual Stimulation

Intellectual stimulation is displayed when transformational leaders engage their teams in decision-making processes to foster creativity, simultaneously fostering autonomy by enabling team members to participate in decisions that impact them (Bass, 1999). Cultivating the creativity of followers is a crucial element in fostering innovation. Equally vital is the leader's communication of the vision to the team, facilitating a shared understanding of goals and the necessary steps for manifesting the envisioned outcomes.

Taylor Swift has a particularly unique way of utilizing intellectual stimulation with her fan base using "Easter eggs" (Atari, 2022), which are hidden clues or messages that she strategically places in her music, social media, and public appearances. These Easter eggs serve as puzzles for her fans to decipher and interpret, revealing insights about her upcoming projects, potential release dates, personal experiences, or artistic themes. The clues can be anything from subtle references in her music videos, the strategic use of capital letters in song titles and social media posts, the number of exclamation marks in a tweet, and even the colors she chooses to wear during her performances. By incorporating these Easter eggs, Swift fosters a sense of community and excitement among her fans, who enjoy the challenge of unraveling the hidden messages and feel a deeper connection to the artist.

Swift's largest and most notable "Easter egg hunt" occurred, September 2023, when the artist partnered with Google to create a series of word scramble puzzles. Once fans collectively solved 33 million puzzles correctly, it unlocked the titles of Swift's vault tracks for her re-recorded album, *1989 (Taylor's Version)*. In an interview with Yahoo Entertainment, Ginnie Low, who runs a Swift-centric TikTok account @TheThriftySwiftie, discussed collective feeling around the puzzles:

> She literally said 33 million puzzles had to be solved – that has to be collaborative ... It brought me genuine joy to see people say things like, "OK, tapping out for the night, time to go to bed ... international Swifties, it's your turn." It was truly this moment of togetherness. (Reilly, 2023)

The clues that are revealed in Swift's Easter eggs typically indicate what is happening *next* for the artist, fostering excitement around the shared vision between the artist (leader) and fans (followers).

Individualized Consideration

Individualized consideration is when a leader focuses on understanding the needs and fostering the growth potential of others (Bass, 1999). They create a nurturing environment that values individual differences, have high interaction with followers, and are attuned to individual follower concerns. Some key indicators of this style are, recognizing different strengths and weaknesses among followers, being an "active" listener, assigning projects based on differing abilities and needs, engaging in two-way communication, and promoting self-development (Kirkbride, 2006).

Taylor Swift has a unique and relatively intimate relationship with her fan base that consists of rich two-way communication. "I'm really in touch with my fans and I know what they like," said Swift in an ABC interview with Barbara Walters in 2014. "I want to come up with as many ways that we can spend time together and bond because it keeps me normal. It keeps my life feeling manageable." The artist has used social media for years to connect with fans directly. Through earnest Instagram posts, popping up in the comments on fans' livestreams, reblogging fans on Tumblr, and candid Twitter interactions, Taylor Swift provides insights into her life and makes her fans feel like they are part of her journey. She has also engaged one-on-one with fans through surprise meet-up events, recruiting fans to dance alongside her in her music videos, and even attending a fan's bridal shower (Tilchen, 2019). In addition, she has aided fans through various financial struggles. She assisted a fan by paying off her student loans (Clark, 2015), donated over $15,000 to a fan whose mother had been in a coma (Tilchen, 2019), and sent nearly $6,000 to a Swiftie who was unable to afford tuition and rent (O'Kane, 2019). These are just a handful of countless stories that fans have shared over the years of Swift's personalized, generous nature.

Swift appears to carry this same level of individual care and concern for those who work for her as well. In 2023, following the end of the first leg of the Eras Tour, Swift awarded over $55 million in bonuses to caterers, truck drivers, dancers, and other workers of the tour crew (Chiu, 2023), including $100,000 bonuses to each of the individual truck drivers. This is not the first time Swift has generously rewarded her team though. In 2015, Swift reportedly took her staff, backup dancers, and crew on all all-expenses paid trip to Australia (Sharma, 2023).

In addition to caring for the individual needs of her fans and employees, Swift seeks to look out for the interests of new and up-and-coming artists. In 2015, Swift squared off with Apple Music over their three-month free trial period offer to customers. Apple had no plans to compensate or pay royalties to artists during customers' free trial period. Swift and numerous other artists found this agreement unfair and, understandably, highly objectionable. Swift issued an open letter to Apple, in which she stated the following quotes:

> *Three months is a long time to go unpaid, and it is unfair to ask anyone to work for nothing ... We don't ask you for free iPhones. Please don't ask us to provide you with our music for no compensation.*

> *This is not about me .... This is about the new artist or band that has just released their first single and will not be paid for its success. This is about the young songwriter who just got his or her first cut and thought that the royalties from that would get them out of debt. This is about the producer who works tirelessly to innovate and create, just like the innovators and creators at Apple are pioneering in their field ... but will not get paid for a quarter of a year's worth of plays on his or her songs. (CBS News, 2015)*

Swift's willingness to stick up for the interests of other artists is yet another display of her individualized consideration skills.

CONCLUSION

In conclusion, Taylor Swift's approach to leadership through resilience, authenticity, and a strong commitment to her vision offers valuable lessons for leaders in any field. By embracing fearlessness, acting ethically, and stimulating intellectual and emotional engagement, leaders can inspire and drive their teams toward achieving remarkable success.

- Leaders who openly address their doubts and challenges can inspire their teams to overcome their own obstacles and strive for greatness.

- Leaders who "walk the walk" gain the trust and respect of their followers, fostering a positive and motivated organizational culture.

- Engaging followers in intellectual stimulation by encouraging creativity and participation in decision-making processes is a key to innovation.

The principles discussed in this chapter demonstrate that transformational leadership, whether applied to individual aspirations or collective goals, is a powerful approach that can drive significant positive change in any context.

REFERENCES

Alexander, J. T. (2023, December 7). *The global impact of Taylor Swift: A musical trailblazer and Cultural Icon.* Medium. https://medium.com/@JT.Alexander/the-global-impact-of-taylor-swift-a-musical-trailblazer-and-cultural-icon-d3777aad612

Atari. (2022, May 7). *So let's talk about that Easter Egg.* Retrieved August 15, 2024, from https://atari.com/blogs/atari/so-let-s-talk-about-that-easter-egg

Avolio, B. J., & Yammarino, F. J. (2002). *Transformational and charismatic leadership: The road ahead.* Elsevier Science.

Barbara Walters Presents: The 10 Most Fascinating People of 2014 special, airing Dec. 14. (2015, June 21). *Taylor Swift pens open letter to Apple about "shocking" policy.* CBS. Retrieved August 15, 2024, from https://www.cbsnews.com/news/taylor-swift-pens-open-letter-to-apple-about-shocking-policy/

Bass, B. (1999). Two decades of research and development in transformational leadership. *European Journal of Work and Organizational Psychology, 8,* 9–32.

Bass, B. M. (1985). *Leadership and performance beyond expectations.* Free Press.

Bass, B. M., & Riggio, R. E. (2006). *Transformational leadership* (2nd ed.). Lawrence Erlbaum Associates.

Boyd, J. T. (1988). *Leadership extraordinary: A cross national military perspective on transactional versus transformational leadership* (Doctoral dissertation). Nova University.

Bulgarella, C. (2023, October 23). Three ways to tap into Taylor Swift's authenticity and build an eras-like workplace. *Forbes.* https://www.forbes.com/sites/caterinabulgarella/2023/10/20/three-ways-to-tap-into-taylor-swifts-authenticity-and-build-an-eras-like-workplace/?sh=1b499f9518b7

CBS News. (2015, June 21). *Taylor Swift pens open letter to Apple about "shocking" policy.* CBS. Retrieved August 15, 2024, from https://www.cbsnews.com/news/taylor-swift-pens-open-letter-to-apple-about-shocking-policy/

Chiu, M. (2023, August 2). Taylor swift gives bonuses totaling over $55 million to every person working on massive eras tour. *People.* Retrieved January 2, 2024, from https://people.com/taylor-swift-gives-bonuses-totaling-55-million-every-person-working-eras-tour-7568556

Clark, C. (2015, January 15). Taylor swift sends superfan $1,989 for student loans. *USA Today.* Retrieved January 2, 2024, from https://www.usatoday.com/story/life/people/2015/01/14/taylor-swift-send-superfan-1989-for-student-loans/21743251/

Curphy, G. J. (1991). *An empirical evaluation of Bass' (1985) theory of transformational and transactional leadership*. University of Minnesota.

Dailey, H. (2022, May 18). Taylor Swift's NYU Commencement speech: Read the full transcript. *Billboard*. https://www.billboard.com/music/music-news/taylor-swift-nyu-commencement-speech-full-transcript-1235072824/

Downton, J. V. (1973). *Rebel leadership: Commitment and charisma in the revolutionary process*. Free Press.

George, B., Sims, P., McLean, A. N., & Mayer, D. (2007). Discovering your authentic leadership. *Harvard Business Review, 85*(2), 129.

Hammond, A. B., Johnson, S. K., Weiner, M. B., & Lerner, J. V. (2022, March 16). From Taylor Swift to MLK: Understanding adolescents' famous character role models. *Journal of Moral Education, 53*(1), 157–175. https://doi.org/10.1080/03057240.2022.2041409

Harter, S. (2002). Authenticity. In C. R. Snyder and S. J. Lopez (Eds.), *Handbook of positive psychology* (pp. 382–394). Oxford University Press.

Kirkbride, P. (2006). Developing transformational leaders: The full range leadership model in action. *Industrial and Commercial Training, 38*(1), 23–32.

Kitur, K., Choge, J., & Tanui, E. (2020). Relationship between principals' transformational leadership style and secondary school students' academic performance in Kenya Certificate of Secondary Education in Bomet County, Kenya. *Universal Journal of Educational Research, 8*(2):402–409.

Luthans, F., & Avolio, B. J. (2003). Authentic leadership development. In K. S. Cameron, J. E. Dutton, & R. E. Quinn (Eds.), *Positive organizational scholarship: Foundations of a new discipline* (pp. 241–258). Berrett-Koehler.

Morgenroth, T., Ryan, M. K., & Peters, K. (2015). The motivational theory of role modeling: How role models influence role aspirants' goals. *Review of General Psychology, 19*(4), 465–483.

O'Kane, C. (2019, August 13). Taylor swift sends fan $6,000 for tuition and rent. *CBS News*. Retrieved January 2, 2024, from https://www.cbsnews.com/news/taylor-swift-sends-fan-6000-for-tuition-and-rent-after-tumblr-post-ayesha-get-learn-girl-money/

Okoli, I., Akpan, U., & Etim, J. (2021). Transformational leadership and its impact on organizational performance in Nigerian higher education institutions. *African Journal of Business and Economic Research, 16*(2), 123–144.

Reilly, K. (2023). *Taylor Swift turns her fans into detectives to solve her puzzles. Swifties wouldn't have it any other way*. Yahoo! https://www.yahoo.com/entertainment/taylor-swift-easter-eggs-puzzles-1989-vault-164224223.html

Schneider, M. (2023, October 30). 9 ways Taylor Swift has changed the Music Business. *Billboard*. https://www.billboard.com/lists/how-taylor-swift-changed-music-business/taylor-swift-artists-rights/

Sharma, A. (2023, September 8). Taylor swift has a lesson for all organisations: Recognize and reward your employees well! *ET HR World.* Retrieved January 2, 2024, from https://hrme.economictimes.indiatimes.com/news/talent-management/taylor-swift-has-a-lesson-for-all-organisations-recognise-reward-your-employees-well/103491407

Swift, T. (2021). Fearless [Song]. *On Fearless* (Taylor's Version). Republic Records.

Tilchen, J. (2019, August 21). *Taylor Swift's fans have known her for 13 years – This is how she's kept growing with them.* MTV. https://www.mtv.com/news/29ig45/taylor-swift-evolution-of-swifties-relationship

4

SPARKS FLY[1]

ABSTRACT

This chapter focuses on creativity and innovation, drawing inspiration from Taylor Swift's song "Sparks Fly." The chapter highlights the distinction between creativity (generating new ideas) and innovation (implementing these ideas). Using Swift's authentic and entrepreneurial leadership style as an example, the chapter demonstrates how leaders can foster a supportive environment that encourages both creativity and innovation. It also explores various leadership behaviors that help cultivate these qualities, emphasizing how leaders can drive organizational success by nurturing creativity and innovation within their teams.

Keywords: Creativity and innovation; authentic leadership; entrepreneurial leadership; leadership and creativity; Taylor Swift leadership

"Sparks Fly" was released on Taylor Swift's original 2010 version of *Speak Now* and again on the re-release in 2023, *Speak Now (Taylor's Version)*. The term "sparks fly" metaphorically captures the essence of creativity, representing the sudden, energetic bursts of inspiration and innovative ideas that ignite the creative process. Subsequently, this chapter focuses on the importance of creativity and innovation in keeping organizations competitive. Although creativity and

---

[1]Swift, T. (2023). Sparks Fly [Song]. *On Speak Now* (Taylor's Version). Republic Records.

innovation are often thought to be the same, they are actually different processes. Creativity is about coming up with new ideas, while innovation is about putting those ideas into action. This chapter looks at how leaders can encourage both creativity and innovation by creating supportive environments. Using Taylor Swift as an example, we'll see how her authentic and entrepreneurial leadership style can inspire others and lead to success. This chapter also discusses the different leadership behaviors that help foster creativity and innovation, showing how leaders can use these traits to help their organizations grow and thrive.

CREATIVITY AND INNOVATION

Professors and organizational leaders alike recognize that creativity and innovation are drivers that allow organizations to maintain their competitive advantage (Anderson et al., 2004; Anderson et al., 2014; Zhou & Shalley, 2003). While most people agree that creativity and innovation are important, it's not always clear how they are different. These two terms are often used interchangeably, but they are actually closely related yet distinct processes.

In a meta-analysis of leadership, creativity, and innovation, authors Hughes et al. (2018) provide additional clarity on the distinct differences between the two processes. Hughes et al. (2018) explain that workplace creativity involves the thought process and actions taken to come up with new ideas. On the other hand, workplace innovation refers to the steps taken to put these new ideas into practice (see Table 1).

Table 1. **Swift's Demonstrated Core Values.**

Feature	Creativity	Innovation
Idea generation	Yes	No
Idea promotion	No	Yes
Idea implementation	No	Yes
Novelty	Absolute novelty: the generation of something "new"	Not necessarily, can be relatively novel, that is, adopting and adapting others' ideas
Utilitarian focus	Not necessarily – creative ideas can be generated with no specific regard to improving organizational outcomes	Necessarily – innovative actions are initiated with the goal of improving organizational outcomes

(Continued)

Table 1. (*Continued*)

Feature	Creativity	Innovation
Where does it take place?	The *processes* involved in creativity are largely intrapersonal and cognitive. Social exchanges can help to refine and improve creative ideas; however, creative *ideas* are by definition cognitive in nature.	The *processes* involved in innovation are largely interpersonal, social, and practical.
What does it result in?	The *product* of a successful creative process is an idea.	The *product* of a successful innovative process is a functioning and implemented idea.

Source: Adapted from Hughes et al. (2018).

Creativity mainly involves individuals exploring and coming up with new and original ideas. Research suggests that for employees to be creative, leaders need to create a safe and motivating environment where employees feel comfortable and inspired to think flexibly (Perry-Smith & Mannucci, 2017).

Innovation, on the other hand, is mainly a team effort that focuses on bringing new ideas to life. These ideas can come from different people, are adjusted to fit the situation, get approval from others, and are finally put into action (Hughes et al., 2018). To encourage innovation, studies suggest that leaders should support their employees and help them take the necessary steps to make these new ideas happen (Perry-Smith & Mannucci, 2017).

LEADERSHIP STYLES AND BEHAVIORS

Certain leadership styles and behaviors play a crucial role in fostering creativity and innovation among followers. Leaders who embrace openness, encourage experimentation, and provide a supportive environment tend to inspire their teams to think creatively, take risks, and explore new ideas. By nurturing a culture that values innovation, these leaders empower their followers to unleash their creative potential and drive organizational growth.

Authentic Leadership Style

Authentic leaders are often characterized as confident, optimistic, transparent, and moral/ethical and give high priority to aiding followers/employees in their own personal development (Luthans & Avolio, 2003). In terms of their leadership style, authentic leaders do not aim to persuade or coerce followers. Instead, authentic leaders use their authentic values, beliefs, and behaviors as models for followers to adopt in their own personal development pursuits (Luthans & Avolio, 2003). They are known for engendering trust and developing genuine connections with others (George et al., 2007). As these authentic leaders develop over time, they tend to become more concerned about serving others than they are about their own accomplishments or recognition (George et al., 2007).

The self-awareness inherent in authentic leadership enables leaders to demonstrate transparency in their actions and "lead by example" (Walumbwa et al., 2008), fostering a culture where followers are encouraged to creatively engage with their tasks (Seibert et al., 2011). Lee et al. (2020) found that authentic leaders appeared to be particularly effective at fostering employee creativity. They determined that authentic leaders are inclined to prioritize the holistic development of their followers, including the cultivation of authenticity among them (e.g., Hoch et al., 2018). This implies that leaders can effectively nurture creativity not only through modeling and encouragement but also by embodying authenticity and trustworthiness (Lee et al., 2020).

Swift has been highly regarded and appreciated for her authenticity throughout the years, remaining true to her own values and beliefs and refusing to compromise her identity to conform to standards set by the music industry (Lafair, 2023). Some of her demonstrated core values include:

- *Kindness and appreciation for fans*: Swift places great importance on kindness and treating her fans with respect and gratitude. In addition to connecting with her fans through her various creative outlets, Swift has expertly handled instances during the Eras Tour when she has spotted fans in the crowd who are in distress or in need of assistance, demonstrating genuine care (Stewart, 2024).

- *Artistic integrity*: Swift maintains creative control and authenticity in her art. She is heavily involved in every aspect of production and is either the sole writer or a co-writer of all of her songs.

- *Equity and inclusivity*: Swift promotes values of equality, tolerance, and acceptance, as reflected in this quote: "*My parents taught me never to judge others based on whom they love, what color their skin is, or their religion*" (Kody, 2009). She has used her platform to advocate for causes like the Equality Act and LGBTQ+ rights.

- *Resilience and hard work*: Despite facing criticism and challenges, Swift has demonstrated resilience and a strong work ethic, emphasizing this core value in public statements such as her NYU graduation speech (Dailey, 2022).

- *Strong family support*: Swift values her close-knit family, frequently involving and thanking her parents and brother throughout her career.

This authentic approach has shown to resonate with fans, fostering trust and inspiration (Lafair, 2023), key elements in promoting creativity among followers.

The Eras Tour has served as the ultimate environment for fans to display their creativity. With each album or "era" serving up its own unique sound, aesthetic, and vibe, Swift rotates through multiple costumes during each concert, with "Swifties" following suit by showing up to shows adorned in outfits that represent their own favorite "era." Reporter for *The New Yorker*, Amanda Petrusich (2023), describes the concert scene as highly fashionable with shimmering outfits, elaborate eye make-up, strangers sharing supportive compliments to one another, and an overall ecstatic energy.

In addition to adorning themselves in their favorite eras' costumes, fans creatively incorporated Swift's lyrics into the concert experience. Taking the lyric "make the friendship bracelets, take the moment and taste it," from Swift's *Midnights* track, "You're on Your Own Kid." Kelly (2024) fans created, accessorized, and traded friendship bracelets with one another throughout each show.

Feeling empowered to express their own creative expression, fans channeled that same energy to create art to connect with the artist directly. During night one of the Eras Tour in Nashville, TN, floor-level fans created posters featuring Swift's late grandmother, Marjorie Finlay, and displayed them for the artist to see as she sang her tribute song "Marjorie." Swift was visibly in awe of the thoughtful display that fans had created (Remillard, 2023).

Ultimately, leadership that emphasizes the development of strong bonds between leaders and followers, marked by a significant level of trust, appears to be the most effective in encouraging employee creativity in much the same way that Taylor Swift inspires creativity among her fans.

Entrepreneurial Leadership

Leaders who use an entrepreneurial leadership style are especially good at encouraging innovative behavior in employees (Hughes et al., 2018). According to Renko et al. (2015), entrepreneurial leadership involves guiding and motivating team members to achieve organizational goals by recognizing and taking advantage of new opportunities. Entrepreneurial leaders are known for their traits and behaviors like being innovative, willing to take risks, proactive, and independent (Sutanto & Eliyana, 2015).

In 2019, Taylor Swift ran face first into adversity when her original music label, Big Machine Records, sold the rights to her original six albums to Scooter Braun, owner and music manager of the private-equity group, Ithaca Holdings. Braun subsequently turned around and sold those masters for $300 million to another company, Shamrock Holdings. Swift was left without any ownership rights to her original work, while Braun would continue to make a profit any time the songs were bought or streamed (Bruner, 2023).

In a March 2021 Instagram post, Swift stated that "Artists should own their own work for so many reasons... But the most screamingly obvious one is that the artist is the only one who really knows that body of work." (Rackham, 2021). Swift was bringing public attention to a long-time controversial practice of the large-scale music industry (Bruner, 2023).

After feuding in court with Braun's team for about a year, in November of 2020, Swift became officially free to re-record her old music. She made her intentions known to fans and they responded positively and in support of the artist. A sentiment tweeted by one fan and echoed by many others was "We all will be deleting all of her old music from our playlists and apps and will only be streaming Taylor's art owned by Taylor" (Frishberg, 2020).

While fans were supportive of Swift's move to re-record her music, Swift wanted to take it a step further by making the fans an intricate part of the re-release process. In a 2019 interview with Entertainment Weekly, Swift discussed her excitement around her fans' theories when it came to decoding her clues or "easter eggs." "I love that they like the cryptic hint-dropping. Because as long as they like it, I'll keep doing it. It's fun. It feels mischievous and playful" (Suskind, 2019).

In anticipation of re-released or newly released albums, Swifties begin dissecting everything Swift says, posts, or wears. Fans have also caught on to Taylor's use of intricate math and coordinating dates when it comes to solving the artist's riddles. For example, many online fans accurately predicted the re-release announcement of Swift's *1989* album, which was announced at her last show of the 2023 U.S. leg of the Eras Tour on August 9th (8/9 or 89). Some die-hard fans noted that the original 1989 album was released on October 27, 2014 and that by releasing it on August 9, 2023 it adds up to 3,208 days in between – 8 years, 9 months, (representing 89 for *1989*) and 13 (13 representing Swift's lucky number) days to be exact (Anonymous, 2023, August 6).

Swift successfully identified and acted upon an entrepreneurial opportunity by making the decision to re-record her old music. She went on to influence her fans to get on board with the plan, which they readily embraced through innovative and collaborative activities and engagement with the artist.

CONCLUSION

In this chapter, we explored how being creative and innovative can help both individuals and organizations succeed, using Taylor Swift's story as an example. Just like how Taylor Swift worked hard to achieve her dreams, leaders can use creativity and innovation to help their teams succeed too. This chapter explored several ideas including:

- Being creative means coming up with new ideas, while being innovative means putting those ideas into action.

- Leaders play a big role in encouraging creativity and innovation in their teams. They can do this by being genuine and trustworthy, like Taylor Swift, and by recognizing and taking advantage of new opportunities.

- Leaders can be entrepreneurial, or willing to take risks for a bigger reward. Swift got her fans involved in the process, which made them feel excited and included.

In summary, Taylor Swift's journey teaches us that creativity and innovation are important for success. By being open-minded and willing to try new things, leaders can inspire their teams to achieve great things together.

REFERENCES

Anderson, N., De Dreu, C. K., & Nijstad, B. A. (2004). The routinization of innovation research: A constructively critical review of the state-of-the-science. *Journal of Organizational Behavior*, 25(2), 147–173.

Anderson, N., Potočnik, K., & Zhou, J. (2014). Innovation and creativity in organizations: A state-of-the-science review, prospective commentary, and guiding framework. *Journal of Management*, 40(5), 1297–1333.

Anonymous. (2023, August 6). *8 years, 9 months, 13 days from 1989 to 1989 [Thread]*. Reddit. https://www.reddit.com/r/TaylorSwift/comments/15nbmdz/8_years_9_months_13_days_from_1989_to_1989/

Bruner, R. (2023). Here's why Taylor Swift is re-releasing her old albums. *Time Magazine*. Retrieved, 2024, from https://time.com/5949979/why-taylor-swift-is-rerecording-old-albums/

Dailey, H. (2022, May 18). Taylor Swift's NYU Commencement speech: Read the full transcript. *Billboard*. https://www.billboard.com/music/music-news/taylor-swift-nyu-commencement-speech-full-transcript-1235072824/

Frishberg, H. (2020). Taylor Swift is finally 'free' to re-record her old hits and fans are hyped. *New York Post*. Retrieved, 2024, from https://nypost.com/2020/11/02/taylor-swift-is-finally-free-to-re-record-her-old-hits-and-fans-are-hyped/

George, B., Sims, P., McLean, A. N., & Mayer, D. (2007). Discovering your authentic leadership. *Harvard Business Review*, 85(2), 129–138.

Hoch, J. E., Bommer, W. H., Dulebohn, J. H., & Wu, D. (2018). Do ethical, authentic, and servant leadership explain variance above and beyond transformational leadership? A meta-analysis. *Journal of Management*, 44, 501–529. https://doi.org/10.1177/0149206316665461

Hughes, D., Lee, A., Tian, A. W., Newman, A., & Legood, A. (2018). Leadership, creativity and innovation: A meta-analytic review. *The Leadership Quarterly*, 29(5), 549–569.

Kelly, S. (2024, August 14). So, this is why Taylor Swift fans wear and swap friendship bracelets at the Era Tour. *Huff Post*. Retrieved August 16, 2024, from https://www.huffingtonpost.co.uk/entry/so-this-is-why-taylor-swift-fans-wear-and-swap-friendship-bracelets-at-the-era-tour_uk_66bb7125e4b0768018b70694

Kody, D. (2009). *Taylor Swift's mission: Take a stand against hate! Seventeen*. Retrieved, 2024, from https://www.seventeen.com/life/school/advice/a3549/mission-taylor-swift/

Lafair, S. (2023). *Here's why Taylor Swift is the perfect icon of a GUTSY WOMEN LEADER*. LinkedIn. https://www.linkedin.com/pulse/heres-why-taylor-swift-perfect-icon-gutsy-women-sylvia-lafair/

Lee, A., Legood, A., Hughes, D., Tian, A. W., Newman, A., & Knight, C. (2020). Leadership, creativity and innovation: A meta-analytic review. *European Journal of Work and Organizational Psychology, 29*(1), 1–35.

Luthans, F., & Avolio, B. J. (2003). Authentic leadership development. In K. S. Cameron, J. E. Dutton, & R. E. Quinn (Eds.), *Positive Organizational Scholarship: Foundations of a New Discipline* (pp. 241–258). Berrett-Koehler.

Perry-Smith, J. E., & Mannucci, P. V. (2017). From creativity to innovation: The social network drivers of the four phases of the idea journey. *Academy of Management Review, 42*(1), 53–79.

Petrusich, A. (2023). The startling intimacy of Taylor Swift's eras tour. *The New Yorker.* https://www.newyorker.com/magazine/2023/06/19/taylor-swift-eras-tour-review

Rackham, A. (2021, November 12). Taylor Swift Red re-release: 'It was the soundtrack to my own break-up'. *BBC News Beat.* Retrieved August 16, 2024, from https://www.bbc.co.uk/news/newsbeat-59264000

Remillard, J. (2023). The 5 best Taylor Swift 'eras tour' fan moments: The NY post weighs in. *New York Post.* Retrieved, 2024, from https://nypost.com/2023/06/01/taylor-swift-eras-tour-fan-moments-2023-where-to-buy-tickets/

Renko, M., El tarabishy, A., Carsrud, A. L., & Brännback, M. (2015). Understanding and measuring entrepreneurial leadership style. *Journal of Small Business Management, 53*(1), 54–74. https://doi.org/10.1111/jsbm.12086

Seibert, S. E., Wang, G., & Courtright, S. H. (2011). Antecedents and consequences of psychological and team empowerment in organizations: A meta-analytic review. *Journal of Applied Psychology, 96*(5), 981.

Stewart, C. (2024). *Taylor Swift stopped her eras show after seeing a fan in distress.* BuzzFeed. https://www.buzzfeed.com/chelseastewart/taylor-swift-pauses-scotland-concert-help-fan

Suskind, A. (2019). New reputation: Taylor Swift shares intel on TS7, fan theories, and her next era. *Entertainment Weekly.* Retrieved, 2024, from https://ew.com/music/2019/05/09/taylor-swift-cover-story/

Sutanto, E. M., & Eliyana, A. (2015). The study of entrepreneurial performance with entrepreneurial leadership and organizational learning capability as antecedent variables in East Java Higher Education, Indonesia. *Academic Research International, 6*(3), 86–104.

Walumbwa, F. O., Avolio, B. J., Gardner, W. L., Wernsing, T. S., & Peterson, S. J. (2008). Authentic leadership: Development and validation of a theory-based measure. *Journal of Management, 34*(1), 89–126.

Zhou, J., & Shalley, C. E. (2003). Research on employee creativity: A critical review and directions for future research. *Research in Personnel and Human Resources Management, 22*, 165–217.

5

ENCHANTED[1]

ABSTRACT

This chapter explores the influence and charisma of Taylor Swift, highlighting her use of power to captivate audiences. The chapter examines the five bases of power – coercive, reward, legitimate, expert, and referent – demonstrated through Swift's strategic actions in the music industry. Swift's ability to inspire, reward, and connect authentically with her audience showcases her remarkable leadership. Swift exemplifies how true power lies in authentic connections and steadfast determination, turning personal stories into widely inspiring and authoritative narratives.

Keywords: Power in leadership; bases of power; charismatic leadership; leadership influence; Taylor Swift influence

In the realm of influence and charisma, few figures are as captivating as Taylor Swift. The term "Enchanted," aptly chosen for this chapter, encapsulates the magical allure and commanding presence Swift holds in the world of music and beyond. Power, in its essence, is about the ability to influence others – a concept embodied by Swift through her strategic use of coercive, reward, legitimate, expert, and referent power. As we explore the multifaceted nature of power, we will uncover how Swift enchants her audience,

---

[1]Swift, T. (2023). Enchanted [Song]. *On Speak Now* (Taylor's Version). Republic Records.

industry peers, and even global markets, transforming her personal narrative into a universal source of inspiration and authority. Through her actions, Swift demonstrates that true power lies not just in positions held but in the enchantment one can weave through authentic connection, unwavering resolve, and remarkable talent.

WHAT IS POWER?

Power is a word that is used often but is not widely understood. When the word power is used, what is really being discussed is influence. More specifically, a person or entity's ability to influence others can include another person(s), a group, or even societal norms. French and Raven (1959) are the most widely cited when it comes to discussing and analyzing power as a means of social influence. The authors defined social influence as "a change in the belief, attitude, or behavior of a person (the target of influence) which results from the action of another person (an influencing agent)" (French & Raven, 1959; Raven, 2004, p. 1242). French and Raven (1959) go on to identify five bases of power which include coercive, reward, legitimate, expert, and referent power.

Coercive Power

Coercive power is when a threat of force or punishment is used to gain compliance. The threat or means of force could be physical, social, emotional, political, and/or economical. As the name implies, this form of power is based on the concept of coercion. Coercion is "the act or process of persuading someone forcefully to do something that they do not want to do" (Coercion, n.d.). For coercion to work effectively, it must be clear to the target that the person or entity making the threat not only has the means or authority to carry it out but is also ready and willing to do so (Raven, 2004). For example, a manager who is supervising a unit that is grossly understaffed will likely not be taken seriously by employees if the manager decided to threaten them with dismissal for noncompliance. While that manager has the authority to carry out the threat, the employees understand that the manager does not have the resources available to carry out said threat.

Taylor Swift has effectively used coercive power in her business negotiations. As previously discussed, Swift entered into contentious negotiations with Spotify, the world's most popular music streaming service, back in 2014 before the initial release of her "1989" album. Swift and her label at the time, Big Machine, requested that Swift's music only be available to the company's paid subscribers. This request was made due to Spotify's two-tier customer business model, which consisted of users who paid a subscription fee to listen to streamed music and users who listen to streamed music for free but included advertisements. Spotify had the practice of paying artists less in royalty payments when the artists' music was streamed using Spotify's free tier (Bacle, 2014).

Spotify initially denied Swift's request to keep her music off the platform's free tier. In response, Swift and her team pulled her entire catalog off the platform. Spotify tried to pressure Swift into coming back to the platform by launching a social media campaign that attempted to get Swift's fans to persuade her to change her mind (Shonk, 2024). Despite these attempts, Swift stood firm and her fans supported her decision. Spotify ultimately conceded and met Swift's demands by changing their business model to raise royalty rates for not just her, but for all artists. Swift was able to successfully force Spotify into complying with her demands using coercive power. She not only had the means to pull her music from the platform, but she was willing to go through with the threat when her initial set of demands were not met (Bacle, 2014).

Reward Power

Reward power exerts influence by using rewards instead of threats and is often considered the opposite of coercive power. Rewards are the promise of monetary or nonmonetary compensation in exchange for compliance (French & Raven, 1959). Within organizations, rewards are traditionally thought of in terms of raises, promotions, desirable work assignments, resources, training opportunities, and praise/recognition. As with coercive power, reward power is only influential so long as the target perceives that the person in power can deliver on the reward promise. For example, supervisors can have a strong influence on which employees get a raise or promotion, but rarely do they have sole control over such decisions. Depending on how much control the supervisor wields over the desired reward will determine how influential they can be when utilizing reward power.

Taylor Swift has a long history of generosity whereby she rewards fans, employees, and communities with thoughtful gifts, sizable donations, and her most valuable resource, her time. In 2024, Billboard outlined a timeline of some of the pop star's most notable acts of generosity (Dailey & Aniftos, 2024). A handful of those acts have been detailed below (see Fig. 2):

Fig. 2. Swift's Recorded Acts of Generosity (Dailey & Aniftos, 2024).

- October 2011: Donated $70,000 worth of new books geared toward children and teens to her hometown library in Reading, Pennsylvania

- September 2012: Wrote and released the song "Ronan" in honor of a young boy who passed away from cancer and pledged all proceeds from the song to cancer research

- January 2015: Offered to help pay off a fan's student loans, sending her a personal note and a $1,989 donation (referencing her 2014 album "1989")

- February 2015: Donated $50,000 in song proceeds to New York City public schools

- June 2020: Sent $1,300 to a Minneapolis fundraiser after seeing a fan's video set to her song "Only the Young"

- December 2020: Donated to an Ohio food bank after a fan set up an elaborate holiday light display to her song "Christmas Tree Farm"

- March 2021: Donated the entire $50,000 goal amount to a GoFundMe for a mother of five whose husband died of COVID-19

- December 2022: Made a "sizable donation" to a pet rescue foundation run by Beth Stern, who then named a foster cat "Angel Taylor" in her honor

- March 2023: Quietly donated to local food banks in Glendale, Arizona and Las Vegas ahead of her Eras Tour stops in those cities

- August 2023: Awarded Eras Tour employees with generous bonuses up to $100,000 each

Raven's (2008) research further reiterates that rewards do not have to be tangible to be powerful. Even simple gestures, such as recognition or praise, can strengthen leader–follower relationships, providing motivation to followers to continue in the good work they are doing. Swift has been known for fostering connections with her fans online through acknowledging their support, praising their personal projects, and amplifying fans' voices and various causes. As one of the richest and most powerful women on earth, Swift has utilized her resources to reward and give back to all those who have helped her achieve her success.

Legitimate Power

Legitimate power comes from a person's role or title within an organization or society, and others comply because they believe the person has the right to exert influence over them. This power comes from the idea that people should listen to those who hold a superior position and are "in charge" whether it's in a formal or informal group (Pierro et al., 2008). For example, a manager might ask an employee to come into work early or stay late, and because of the manager's position within the organization, the employee is likely to comply, regardless of how the employee personally feels about the request.

Taylor Swift's successful career has granted her a significant level of legitimate power within the music industry and beyond. The singer–songwriter has received a record number of awards and honorifics, including the most award-winning artist for both the American Music Awards (Sanchez, 2022) and the Billboard Music Awards (Grein, 2023), the most Album of the Year Grammy Awards (Willman, 2024), Time Magazine's 2023 Person of the Year Award (Lansky, 2023), and countless others.

In addition to her musical impact, Swift shows the potential to have great political impact as well. A single Instagram post made by Swift encouraging her followers to register to vote to make their voices heard in upcoming elections resulted in a 35,000-person surge in new-voter registration (Sullivan, 2023). Swift's potential to influence voters by either endorsing or denouncing a given political candidate has generated significant discourse in the media and online (Otte, 2024). We argue, along with others, that Swift herself could hold an official position of power within politics one day due to her immense popularity. People worldwide recognize characteristics like empathy, kindness, and a willingness to use power and influence to empower others (Thomas, 2024) in Swift that are often lacking in other political and global leaders. Citizens are "...desperate for leaders that truly care for the most vulnerable and use their platform, moral compass and power to inspire people" (Thomas, 2024). We agree that this is a sentiment shared by many and would most certainly put Swift in a position of political power if she ever chose to enter that space.

Regardless of anyone's opinion of Swift, there is no denying that her views and actions carry authority and weight in multiple spheres of influence. Time magazine's 2023 Person of the Year article summarized it best stating that, "To discuss her movements felt like discussing politics or the weather – a language spoken so widely it needed no context. She became the main character of the world" (Lansky, 2023).

Expert Power

Expert power is derived from what one knows, that is, the person's skill, knowledge, experiences, and/or special talents. When others perceive a person's skillset as specialized or rare, they can influence others more effectively because their expertise is highly regarded (French & Raven, 1959). We often witness this in professions that are highly specialized and where it is difficult or impossible to reproduce their work without an equivalent level of expertise. For example, when a person is diagnosed with a life-altering disease, they will likely seek out a doctor who is highly regarded as an expert in their field and specializes in working with patients with the same or similar diagnoses. The professional opinion of the doctor who is a specialist is more highly valued because of the specialist's perceived expertise (i.e., expert power).

We see this same phenomenon play out in organizations. Expert leaders and managers are thought to be especially influential when leading employees within organizations that are knowledge-intensive (Goodall & Bäker, 2014). Knowledge workers are thought to be more intrinsically motivated and driven by curiosity, as opposed to simply extrinsically motivated by factors such as money (Amabile, 1993, 1996). Expert leaders originate from the field itself and, therefore, tend to understand the value systems, incentives, and core motivations of employees within the field better than managers without core experience within the field (Goodall & Bäker, 2014). Expert leaders also tend to appear more credible and, therefore, command respect and authority due to their proven track record (e.g., Bass, 1985; Bennis & Nanus, 1985; Kouzes & Posner, 2003).

Taylor Swift is undoubtedly an expert in her industry. Not only is she an exceptional singer and performer, but she writes and/or co-writes all her music (Bueti, 2024). Harvard English Professor and poet, Stephanie Burt, discusses that quality of Swift's songwriting in an interview with the Harvard Gazette:

> *She has a terrific ear in terms of how words fit together. She has a sense both of writing songs that convey a feeling that can make you imagine this is the songwriter's own feelings, like in "We Are Never Ever Getting Back Together," and a way of telling stories and creating characters. She can write songs that take place at one moment, and she can write songs where the successive verses give you a series of events, like in "Betty" or "Fifteen."* Stephanie Burt in an interview with the Harvard Gazette (Pazzanese, 2024).

In addition to the numerous awards that have already been mentioned, Swift continues to make music history by breaking long-standing records set by some of the greatest artists of all time. In early 2024, Swift broke one of music's longest standing records for Most Weeks in Billboard 200's Top 10 List, which had previously been held by the Beatles for the past 60 years (Caulfield, 2024). 16 of her albums have reached and maintained top 10 status for a cumulative 384 weeks, surpassing the Beatles' previous record of 382 weeks (Caulfield, 2024).

Taylor Swift exudes expert power due to her exceptional skills and knowledge within the music industry, demonstrated by her prowess as a singer, performer, and songwriter. Her ability to write or co-write all her music showcases her specialized talent, earning her widespread recognition and respect among fans and industry peers. Swift's continual groundbreaking achievements, such as breaking long-standing records previously held by iconic artists like the Beatles (Caulfield, 2024), further solidify her position as an expert in her field, commanding unparalleled credibility, authority, and influence.

Referent Power

Referent power, also known as personal power, stems from the respect and admiration that an individual accrues from others over time. It is characterized by individuals who possess qualities such as charisma, social skills, energy, and vision, which naturally endow them with influence irrespective of other sources of power (Bolman & Deal, 2008). People with referent power are often seen as role models or charismatic leaders (Nikoloski, 2015) who inspire and motivate others through their actions, behavior, and values. An example of a manager effectively utilizing referent power within an organization could be seen in a team leader who is highly respected and admired by their team members due to their charisma, empathy, and ability to inspire. The leader's positive attitude, genuine interest in the well-being of their team, and ability to foster a sense of camaraderie create a work environment where employees feel valued and motivated to perform at their best. As a result, team members willingly follow their lead, not only because of their formal authority but also because of the genuine admiration and respect they have earned from their team.

Out of all the bases of power one can have, referent power may be Taylor Swift's strongest. Clinical fellow in psychology at MGH and Harvard Medical School, Alexandra Gold, discusses the strong social and emotional bond that fans have with Swift, indirectly discussing Swift's referent power:

> *"She is a role model. She is a great example of someone who sticks to their values and shows their fan base that they can reach their goals, whatever those might be. For instance, she's claiming ownership of her work and has been successful in putting out re-recordings [of her older albums] and doing that despite barriers or obstacles that might be in the way. Seeing someone do something like that could be inspiring for a lot of young people."* Alexandra Gold in an interview with the Harvard Gazette (Pazzanese, 2024).

As a highly successful singer–songwriter, Swift has amassed a large and dedicated fan base who deeply admire and respect her. She embodies relatability and vulnerability in her music, often drawing from personal experiences and emotions, which resonates with her fans. Swift's genuine interactions with her audience, both in person and through social media, foster a strong sense of connection and loyalty among her fans. Additionally, her philanthropic efforts and advocacy work further enhance her image as a role model and influential figure. Overall, Taylor Swift's referent power lies in her ability to inspire and influence others through her authenticity, relatability, and genuine connection with her audience.

CONCLUSION

Taylor Swift exudes all five bases of power, showcasing her remarkable influence and impact across various spheres. In this chapter, we explored the following.

- Leaders who cultivate emotional connections with their audience or team can create deep loyalty and trust. By prioritizing genuine relationships over hierarchical authority, leaders can build a strong foundation of support.

- Effective leaders understand that power is multifaceted and requires strategic application. Using coercion, rewards, expertise, and legitimate authority appropriately, while ensuring alignment with ethical principles, allows leaders to navigate complex challenges.

- Demonstrating expertise and maintaining a high standard of performance are essential for building credibility and authority. Leaders who continually refine their skills and knowledge are better positioned to command respect and influence others.

Understanding the various forms of power and using them ethically is essential for responsible leadership. Leaders must recognize the different ways they can influence others – whether through authority, expertise, rewards, or emotional connections – and choose approaches that align with ethical standards and long-term objectives. Misusing power can undermine trust, create resistance, and damage relationships, while responsible application fosters respect and cooperation. By balancing strategy with integrity, leaders can achieve their goals while maintaining credibility and supporting the well-being of those they lead.

REFERENCES

Amabile, T. M. (1993). Motivational synergy: Toward new conceptualizations of intrinsic and extrinsic motivation in the workplace. *Human Resource Management*, 3(3), 185–201.

Amabile, T. M. (1996). Attributions of creativity: What are the consequences? *Creativity Research Journal*, 8(4), 423–426.

Bacle, A. (2014, November 13). Taylor Swift vs. Spotify: A timeline. *Entertainment Weekly*. https://ew.com/article/2014/11/13/taylor-swift-spotify-timeline/

Bass, B. M. (1985). *Leadership and performance beyond expectation*. Free Press.

Bennis, W. G., & Nanus, B. (1985). *Leaders*. Harper & Row.

Bolman, L., & Deal, T. (2008). *Reframing organizations artistry, choice and leadership* (4th ed.). Jossey-Bass.

Bueti, G. (2024). Does Taylor Swift really write her own songs – Daily telegraph. *The DailyTelegraph*. https://www.dailytelegraph.com.au/entertainment/music/does-taylor-swift-really-write-her-own-songs/news-story/0ecab3761b8aa961b6e391a17fac352f

Caulfield, K. (2024). Taylor Swift passes the Beatles for most weeks in Billboard 200's top 10in last 60 years. *Billboard*. https://www.billboard.com/music/chart-beat/taylor-swift-passes-the-beatles-most-weeks-billboard-200-top-10-60-years-1235615209/

Coercion. (n.d.). *Collins COBUILD advanced learner's English dictionary*. Retrieved March 19th, 2024, from https://www.collinsdictionary.com/us/dictionary/english/coercion

Dailey, H., & Aniftos, R. (2024, February 16). A timeline of Taylor Swift's generosity. *Billboard*. https://www.billboard.com/lists/taylor-swifts-charity-donations-gifts-timeline/february-2016-swift-supports-kesha-with-250000/

French, J. R. P., Jr., & Raven, B. H. (1959). The bases of social power. In D. Cartwright (Ed.), *Studies in social power* (pp. 150–167). Institute for Social Research.

Goodall, A. H., & Bäker, A. (2014). A theory exploring how expert leaders influence performance in knowledge-intensive organizations. In I. M. Welpe, J. Wollersheim, S. Ringelhan, & M. Osterloh (Eds.), *Incentives and performance: Governance of research organizations* (pp. 49–67). Springer International Publishing.

Grein, P. (2023, November 20). After the 2023 Billboard Music Awards, who is the all-time biggest winner?. *Billboard*. https://www.billboard.com/music/awards/taylor-swift-drake-billboard-music-awards-tie-1235490009

Kouzes, J. M., & Posner, B. Z. (2003). *Credibility: How leaders gain and lose it, why people demand it*. Jossey-Bass.

Lansky, S. (2023). Time person of the year 2023: Taylor Swift. *Time*. Retrieved, 2024, from fromhttps://time.com/6342806/person-of-the-year-2023-taylor-swift/

Nikoloski, K. (2015). Charismatic leadership and power: Using the power of charisma for better leadership in the enterprises. *Journal of Process Management and New Technologies*, 3(2), 18–26.

Otte, J. (2024). "She could absolutely change my mind": Readers on Taylor Swift's political influence. *The Guardian*. https://www.theguardian.com/music/2024/feb/06/taylor-swift-political-voting-election-influence

Pazzanese, C. (2024). So what exactly makes Taylor Swift so great?. *Harvard. Gazette*.https://news.harvard.edu/gazette/story/2023/08/so-what-exactly-makes-taylor-swift-so-great/

Pierro, A., Cicero, L., & Raven, B. H. (2008). Motivated compliance with bases of social power. *Journal of Applied Social Psychology, 38*(7), 1921–1944.

Raven, B. H. (2004). Power, six bases of. Encyclopedia of Leadership (pp. 1242–1249). Sage.

Raven, B. H. (2008). The bases of power and the power/interaction model of interpersonal influence. *Analyses of Social Issues and Public Policy, 8*(1), 1–22.

Sanchez, R. (2022). Taylor Swift makes AMAS history as most-awarded artist with 40. *Harper's Bazaar*. https://www.harpersbazaar.com/celebrity/latest/a42023886/taylor-swift-2022-american-music-awards-history-most-awarded-artist/

Shonk, K. (2024). *The importance of power in negotiations: Taylor Swift shakes it off*. Harvard Program on Negotiation. https://www.pon.harvard.edu/daily/dispute-resolution/dispute-resolution-with-spotify-taylor-swift-shakes-it-off/

Sullivan, B. (2023). *A Taylor Swift Instagram post helped drive a surge in voter registration*. NPR. https://www.npr.org/2023/09/22/1201183160/taylor-swift-instagram-voter-registration

Thomas, B. (2024, March 4). Taylor swift would get my vote if she ran for office because of how she uses her platform. *The Tennessean*. Retrieved, 2024, from https://www.tennessean.com/story/opinion/contributors/2024/03/04/taylor-swift-grammy-award-winning-icon-presidential-election-moral-character/72845350007/

Willman, C. (2024). Taylor Swift breaks the record for most album of the year Grammy wins, as "midnights" makes it four. *Variety*. https://variety.com/2024/music/news/taylor-swift-album-year-grammys-1235897350/

6

SPEAK NOW[1]

ABSTRACT

This chapter explores Taylor Swift's leadership in music and business. Highlighting her use of leader–member exchange (LMX) and servant leadership (Dansereau et al., 1975), Swift creates a deep connection with her fans. This chapter demonstrates how Swift empowers her fans through open communication, mutual respect, and shared goals. By fostering high-quality relationships and embodying servant leadership traits such as empathy and stewardship, Swift inspires loyalty and trust. Her high level of engagement with her followers turns her influence into a powerful tool for advocating her values and making impactful decisions.

Keywords: Leader–member exchange; servant leadership; empowering leadership; effective communication in leadership; Taylor Swift leadership

In the dynamic worlds of music, entertainment, and business, effective leadership goes beyond talent and charisma; it requires the ability to make decisions that resonate deeply with a diverse and dedicated group. Taylor Swift exemplifies this leadership, using her authority not just to guide, but to empower her fans through strong leader–member exchanges and servant leadership.

---

[1]Swift, T. (2023). Speak Now [Song]. *On Speak Now* (Taylor's Version). Republic Records.

By fostering open communication and aligning her choices with the shared goals of her fan base, Swift creates a sense of mutual respect and trust. The title "Speak Now" reflects Swift's proactive stance in leveraging her influence to voice important decisions and advocate for her values. This chapter explores how her actions embody key leadership theories, demonstrating fairness, transparency, and empathy. Through these practices, Swift not only gains unwavering support but also illustrates the profound impact of empowering leadership.

LEADER–MEMBER EXCHANGE THEORY

LMX theory, first introduced by Dansereau et al. (1975), is a leadership concept that emphasizes the one-on-one relationships between leaders and their team members. According to this theory, leaders build unique relationships with each team member, and these relationships can differ in their level of trust, respect, and support. High-quality LMX relationships are marked by strong mutual trust, respect, and a sense of obligation, while low-quality LMX relationships tend to lack these positive features (Dansereau et al., 1975).

LMX theory explains that leaders develop different types of relationships with their team members based on their interactions. When leaders have high-quality exchanges with their team members, those members tend to be more committed, satisfied, and productive. On the other hand, low-quality exchanges can cause team members to become disengaged and perform poorly. The quality of these relationships has a big impact on the organization, affecting things like job satisfaction, the likelihood of employees leaving, and positive behaviors that go beyond their job requirements (Graen & Uhl-Bien, 1995).

So, what differentiates "high-quality" from "low-quality" exchanges when it comes to leaders and followers? Followers who have high-quality exchanges/relationships with their leaders are often defined as being within the leader's *in-group*. These relationships are characterized by mutual trust, respect, and a high level of interaction and support. Members of the in-group often receive more attention, resources, and opportunities from the leader. They are typically more involved in decision-making processes and have greater autonomy in their roles. As a result, in-group members are usually more satisfied with their jobs, exhibit higher levels of commitment and performance, and are more likely to engage in organizational citizenship behaviors (Dansereau et al., 1975; Graen & Uhl-Bien, 1995).

Out-groups, on the other hand, consist of members who have lower-quality exchanges/relationships with the leader. These relationships are generally more formal and based strictly on the contractual obligations of the job. Out-group members receive less support, fewer resources and have limited access to decision-making processes. They are often assigned more routine, less challenging tasks and have less frequent and less meaningful interactions with the leader. Consequently, out-group members may experience lower job satisfaction, reduced motivation, and higher turnover intentions (Dansereau et al., 1975; Graen & Uhl-Bien, 1995).

Leaders can mitigate these negative effects by striving to develop high-quality relationships with a larger proportion of their team members (or followers), subsequently reducing the disparity between in-groups and out-groups. This approach fosters a more inclusive and supportive work environment, ultimately benefiting the entire organization (Gerstner & Day, 1997).

In the context of Taylor Swift, the in-group consists of her most dedicated and engaged fans, commonly known as "Swifties." These fans have developed a high-quality relationship with Swift through various means. Direct social media interactions have helped Swift to foster strong relationships with her in-group for years. Swift often interacts directly with fans on social media platforms like Twitter and Instagram. She replies to their comments, likes their posts, and sometimes even surprises them with personal messages (Ian, 2024b). This direct engagement fosters a sense of closeness and belonging among these fans, making them feel like valued members of her online community (Ian, 2024a).

Swift invites select fans to exclusive events, such as secret listening parties for her new albums (known as "Secret Sessions") (e.g., Duboff, 2014; Kelley, 2017). By providing exclusive opportunities, Swift creates an in-group dynamic where these fans receive more attention and resources, enhancing their commitment and satisfaction. These fans get a personal and intimate experience with Swift, further solidifying their loyalty and connection.

Swift has been known to send personalized gifts and handwritten notes to some fans, acknowledging their support and celebrating important milestones in their lives. One such example of this was when Swift sent a handwritten note and gifts to a fan, Andy Mooney, who successfully completed his PhD amidst the 2020 COVID-19 pandemic. Swift's note to Mooney read:

> *...I saw how supportive you've been of my music over the years and was so touched. Thank you so much. I'm also so proud of you for the bravery you've shown in your personal life, choosing to live and love honestly even when it isn't easy. I hope you're doing well in and amongst the chaos we're all living through right now. In these times, I think it's important to revel in the great moments when we can, and this is a moment worth celebrating! Sending you my love and best wishes, Taylor.* (Clarke, 2020).

This personalized approach aligns with the characteristics of high-quality LMX relationships, where mutual respect and personal connection are paramount. Swift's out-group consists of the public and casual fans who have less direct interaction with Swift and do not receive the same level of engagement and personal attention.

While some studies of LMX only categorize followers as either in-group or out-group members, Graen and Uhl-Bien's (1995) paper outlines and acknowledges the evolution of follower relationships through *three* phases: *stranger*, *acquaintance*, and *partner*. These phases can be creatively adapted to describe the relationship between Taylor Swift and her fans using the terms *hater*, *casual listener*, and *Swiftie*.

In the initial phase, a "hater" represents someone who has minimal or negative interactions with Taylor Swift's music. This phase is characterized by a lack of trust and understanding. Haters might have heard of Taylor Swift but don't engage with her music, possibly harboring misconceptions or prejudices. They might criticize her music without fully understanding it, based on surface-level observations or societal stereotypes. There is a clear distance between Taylor and these individuals similar to the formal and distant relationship in the stranger phase of LMX theory (Graen & Uhl-Bien, 1995).

The second phase, corresponding to the acquaintance stage (Graen & Uhl-Bien, 1995), is where individuals transition into "casual listeners." Casual listeners start to hear Taylor's songs more frequently, perhaps on the radio or through friends. They might recognize a few hits and begin to appreciate her talent. Their initial biases start to fade as they get more familiar with her music and her persona, seeing her as a credible artist. While not fully

Table 2.   Phases in Leadership Making Using Taylor Swift.

Phase 1	Phase 2	Phase 3
Hater (stranger)	Casual listener (acquaintance)	Swiftie (partner)
Minimal interactions; lack of trust or understanding; relationships are formal and distant; low-quality exchanges	Increased reciprocal influence; increased interaction, trust, and respect; exchanges are a mix of high and low quality	Influence is highly reciprocal between leader and follower; interactions characterized by mutual respect, trust, and obligation; high-quality exchanges

Adapted from Graen and Uhl-Bien (1995).

invested, casual listeners might attend a concert or add a few of her songs to their playlists, reflecting a growing but still limited engagement.

The final phase, paralleling the partner stage, is where fans become "Swifties." Swifties are deeply engaged with Taylor Swift's music and career. They follow her on social media, attend concerts, and purchase albums and merchandise. They have a thorough understanding and appreciation of her artistry, often defending her against criticism and celebrating her achievements. The relationship is marked by a strong sense of loyalty and connection, where Swifties feel a personal bond with Taylor, often feeling like they are part of a community that she values and acknowledges.

Just as LMX theory emphasizes the development of mutual trust and respect from the stranger to the partner phase, Swifties have built a relationship based on deep admiration and support for Taylor Swift. Taylor Swift often acknowledges her fans' loyalty, much like a leader in the partner phase recognizing and rewarding their team members. This reciprocal relationship enhances the bond and commitment on both sides (see Table 2). In summary, transitioning from a "hater" to a "Swiftie" mirrors the progression in the LMX theory from an impersonal stranger relationship to a deep, trusting partnership. Each phase represents an increasing level of engagement, understanding, and mutual respect.

SERVANT LEADERSHIP

The term "servant leadership" was coined by Robert K. Greenleaf in his 1970 essay "The Servant as Leader." Greenleaf (1970) described servant leadership as a model where the leader's main focus is to serve in contrast to traditional leadership where the main focus is the success of the organization or the leader themselves. According to Greenleaf, a servant leader is someone who is a servant first and chooses to lead as a way to better serve others, ensuring that other people's highest priority needs are being met (Greenleaf, 1970).

This concept emphasizes the well-being, development, and empowerment of followers, as well as the building of a strong community. Servant leaders prioritize the needs of their followers, seeking to support them in achieving their potential and fostering a culture of trust and collaboration. Larry Spears, former president of the Robert K. Greenleaf Center for Servant Leadership, defined the 10 most important characteristics of servant leaders (listed in Table 3):

Table 3. Servant Leader Characteristics According to Robert K. Greenleaf Center for Servant Leadership.

Servant Leader Characteristics	Characteristic Descriptions
Listening	Servant leaders actively listen to the needs and concerns of others, ensuring they understand and address their followers' needs
Empathy	They demonstrate empathy, understanding, and compassion toward others, fostering a supportive and nurturing environment
Healing	Servant leaders seek to heal and help followers overcome personal and professional challenges, promoting their overall well-being
Awareness	They have a high level of self-awareness and situational awareness, which helps them understand and address the complexities within their organization and community
Persuasion	Rather than relying on authority, servant leaders use persuasion and influence to gain cooperation and commitment from others
Conceptualization	They have the ability to conceptualize and envision the future, balancing short-term objectives with long-term goals
Foresight	Servant leaders use foresight to anticipate potential outcomes and make decisions that benefit their followers and the organization in the long run
Stewardship	They act as stewards, taking responsibility for the well-being of their organization and ensuring that resources are used effectively and ethically
Commitment to the growth of people	Servant leaders are dedicated to the personal and professional growth of their followers, providing opportunities for development and empowerment
Building community	They foster a sense of community and belonging, encouraging collaboration and collective action

Adapted from Spears (2010).

Taylor Swift has effectively used her voice and platform to bring awareness to several issues that impact her followers and various marginalized
communities. Swift has exemplified a number of the key characteristics of
servant leadership in her efforts to empower and improve the overall well-
being of these communities.

Swift has been an active listener and displayed a great sense of the empathy for the LGBTQ+ community. Swift spoke out against those that are
critical of the LGBTQ+ community in her song *"You Need to Calm Down"*
(Flam, 2023) and has shown a commitment to fostering growth within that
community by making significant financial contributions to the Tennessee
Equality Project (TEP), an organization that lobbies Tennessee lawmakers
on LGBTQ+ issues (Aviles, 2019). TEP executive director, Chris Sanders,
stated in a 2019 Facebook post that *"Taylor Swift has been a long-time ally
to the LGBTQ community. She sees our struggle in Tennessee and continues
to add her voice with so many good people, including religious leaders, who
are speaking out for love in the face of fear"* (Aviles, 2019).

By publicly speaking out about sexual assault, Swift provides support and
healing for survivors. Swift was involved in a high-profile sexual assault case
against former radio host David Mueller. In 2013, during a meet-and-greet
event before one of Swift's concerts in Denver, Mueller was accused of groping Swift's buttocks during a photo op (Flangan & Campbell, 2017). Swift's
team reported the incident to Mueller's employer KYGO radio, leading to his
termination. Mueller sued Swift in 2015, claiming he was falsely accused and
sought $3 million in damages for slander and interference with his employ-
ment contract (Mueller v. Swift, 2017). Swift countersued Mueller for sexual
assault, seeking only $1 in symbolic damages to serve as an example for
other assault victims (Flanagan & Campbell, 2017). After a highly publi-
cized trial in 2017, a Denver jury unanimously ruled in Swift's favor, finding
that Mueller had groped her and awarding her the $1 in damages she had
requested. The judge also dismissed Mueller's claims against Swift, ruling he
had failed to prove she set out to have him fired (Flanagan, 2017). Swift's
actions encourage others to come forward and seek justice, demonstrating
her role in promoting the emotional and psychological well-being of others,
and specifically, victims of sexual assault.

Swift has served as a steward of the music industry through her advocacy and fight for artists' rights, most notably through her open letter to
Apple (McIntyre, 2015) and her stand against the acquisition of her master

recordings (Prior, 2019). By making these public stands, Swift shows her commitment to protecting and advocating for herself and fellow artists. Her power and influence within the music industry have enabled her to create change toward fostering a fairer and more ethical environment for all artists.

Taylor Swift's efforts to encourage voter registration among her followers helps build a sense of community and collective responsibility, emphasizing the importance of each individual's role in society. In September 2023, Swift made an Instagram post stating that *"I've heard you raise your voices, and I know how powerful they are. Make sure you're ready to use them in our elections this year!"* along with a link to the nonpartisan nonprofit, Vote.org. According to the organization, this resulted in over 35,000 voter registrations, with a significant increase in registrations among young, first-time voters (Sullivan, 2023). Swift empowers her followers, particularly young people, to participate in the democratic process. This action aligns with the servant leadership goal of developing and empowering others to take initiative and lead.

Through her advocacy for LGBTQ+ rights, vocal support for sexual assault survivors, stewardship in the music industry, and efforts to mobilize voter registration, Swift consistently demonstrates a commitment to serving and empowering others. Her ability to listen, empathize, and act in ways that promote healing, growth, and community-building highlights her dedication to the well-being and development of her followers. Swift's servant leadership not only addresses the immediate needs of various communities but also fosters a culture of trust, collaboration, and collective responsibility. By using her platform to advocate for marginalized groups and encourage civic engagement, Swift sets a powerful example of how leaders can inspire and uplift others through selfless service and ethical stewardship.

CONCLUSION

Taylor Swift effectively empowers her fans through strong leader-member exchanges and servant leadership. This approach has helped her to connect deeply with her fans and achieve unprecedented success throughout her career. This chapter explored several ideas, including:

- The importance of strong leader-member exchanges in fostering open communication and aligning with the shared goals of followers.

- The role of personalized engagement in building high-quality leader-member exchanges, leading to greater loyalty, satisfaction, and performance among followers.

- The profound impact of servant leadership on building a strong sense of community among followers and empowering them to succeed.

These lessons can be applied to business leadership, emphasizing the value of fostering strong relationships, personalizing engagement, and prioritizing the well-being and development of team members to create a supportive and high-performing organizational culture.

REFERENCES

Aviles, G. (2019). Taylor Swift donates $113,000 to defeat Tennessee's "slate of hate" bills. *NBC News*. Retrieved from https://www.nbcnews.com/feature/nbc-out/taylor-swift-donates-113-000-defeat-tennessee-s-slate-hate-n992471

Clarke, P. (2020). Taylor Swift sends gifts and handwritten note to a fan completing his PhD. *NME*. Retrieved from https://www.nme.com/news/music/taylor-swift-sends-gifts-and-handwritten-note-to-a-fan-completing-his-phd-2742713

Dansereau, F., Graen, G., & Haga, W. J. (1975). A vertical dyad linkage approach to leadership within formal organizations: A longitudinal investigation of the role making process. *Organizational Behavior and Human Performance, 13*(1), 46–78.

Duboff, J. (2014). Taylor Swift invited hundreds of fans into her home for cookies and dancing. *Vanity Fair*. Retrieved from https://www.vanityfair.com/hollywood/2014/10/taylor-swift-1989-secret-sessions-video

Flam, C. (2023, June 3). Taylor Swift rallies against anti-LGBTQ+ legislation at Chicago concert: 'We Can't Talk About Pride Without Talking About Pain'. *Variety*. Retrieved August 19, 2024, from https://variety.com/2023/music/news/taylor-swift-says-her-concerts-safe-celebratory-space-lgbtq-community-1235632178/

Flanagan, A. (2017). *Taylor Swift wins sexual assault lawsuit against former radio host*. National Public Radio (NPR). Retrieved from https://www.npr.org/sections/therecord/2017/08/14/543473684/taylor-swift-wins-sexual-assault-lawsuit-against-former-radio-host

Flanagan, A., & Campbell, B. (2017). *Judge dumps lawsuit against Taylor Swift, filed by man accused of groping her*. National Public Radio (NPR). Retrieved from https://www.npr.org/sections/therecord/2017/08/11/542873672/judge-dumps-lawsuit-against-taylor-swift-filed-by-man-accused-of-groping-her

Gerstner, C. R., & Day, D. V. (1997). Meta-analytic review of leader-member exchange theory: Correlates and construct issues. *Journal of Applied Psychology*, 82(6), 827–844.

Graen, G. B., & Uhl-Bien, M. (1995). Relationship-based approach to leadership: Development of leader–member exchange (LMX) theory of leadership over 25 years: Applying a multi-level multi-domain perspective. *Leadership Quarterly*, 6(2), 219–247.

Greenleaf, R. K. (1970). *The servant as leader*. Robert K. Greenleaf Publishing Center.

Ian. (2024a). *Taylor Swift's social media strategy: Leveraging platforms for business success*. https://press.farm/taylor-swifts-social-media-strategy-for-success/

Ian. (2024b). *Taylor Swift's marketing strategies: How she connects with fans*. https://press.farm/taylor-swifts-marketing-strategies-with-fans/

Kelley, C. (2017). Taylor Swift hosts 'Reputation' secret sessions listening party at Rhode Island home. *Billboard*. https://www.billboard.com/music/pop/taylor-swift-reputation-secret-session-rhode-island-8006658/

McIntyre, H. (2015). Taylor Swift's letter to Apple: stern, polite, and necessary. *Forbes*. https://www.forbes.com/sites/hughmcintyre/2015/06/21/taylor-swifts-letter-to-apple-stern-polite-and-necessary/?sh=69e71f45113d

Mueller v. Swift. (D. Colo. 2017, May 31). Civil Action No. 15-cv-1974-WJM-KLM.

Prior, R. (2019). When it comes to artists losing the rights to their songs, Taylor Swift is hardly alone. *CNN Business*. Retrieved from https://www.cnn.com/2019/07/01/business/taylor-swift-rights-trnd/index.html

Sullivan, B. (2023). *A Taylor Swift Instagram post helped drive a surge in voter registration*. National Public Radio (NPR). https://www.npr.org/2023/09/22/1201183160/taylor-swift-instagram-voter-registration

7

THE STORY OF US[1]

ABSTRACT

This chapter examines Taylor Swift's exceptional team-building and sustaining efforts that enhance her brand. Using social capital and Hackman's team effectiveness model (Hackman, 1987, 2002, 2009), the chapter delves into how Swift surrounds herself with talented professionals and forms strategic relationships with emerging musicians. These connections foster trust, reciprocity, and collaborative success. By aligning her team with shared goals and maintaining strong interpersonal relationships, Swift exemplifies effective leadership in the music industry. This chapter provides insights into building and managing high-performing teams through unity and shared purpose.

Keywords: Social capital theory; team effectiveness model; high-performing teams; talent management; strategic partnerships

In this chapter, we delve into Taylor Swift's remarkable ability to cultivate and sustain an exceptional team that not only supports her artistic endeavors but also enhances her brand. Through the lens of social capital and Hackman's team effectiveness model, this chapter explores how Swift surrounds herself with talented professionals who promote her, produce her concerts, and perform

---

[1]Swift, T. (2023). The Story of Us [Song]. *On Speak Now* (Taylor's Version). Republic Records.

alongside her. Additionally, we examine her strategic relationships with emerging musicians, whose development and collaboration further bolster her brand. The title "The Story of Us" reflects the collaborative journey and the dynamic relationships Swift has built with her team, highlighting the importance of unity and shared purpose in achieving success. In this chapter, readers will gain insights into the critical elements of building and managing a high-performing team, as exemplified by one of the most successful artists of our time.

SOCIAL CAPITAL THEORY

Social capital theory is used in many fields like sociology, political science, education, and management to understand different experiences and events. Management scholars Leana and Buren (1999) describe social capital as a resource that shows the quality of social relationships within an organization. This theory is based on the idea that relationships and social networks are valuable. It suggests that our connections with others can give us access to resources, information, and opportunities that can help us both personally and professionally (Obstfeld, 2023).

At its core, social capital refers to the value that comes from the networks of relationships, shared norms, and trust within a community, group, or organization (Putnam et al., 1994). It encompasses the following key elements: (see Fig. 3)

- *Networks*: The connections and relationships an individual has with others. A larger, more diverse network provides greater social capital.

- *Trust*: The confidence and reliability that exist within relationships. Higher levels of trust facilitate cooperation and information sharing.

- *Norms of reciprocity*: The mutual expectations and obligations that govern the exchange of resources or favors within a network.

In addition, social capital is categorized into two main types, known as *bonding* social capital and *bridging* social capital (see Fig. 4).

- *Bonding social capital*: This is the value that comes from close relationships with family and close friends. These ties provide emotional support and access to information that is often limited and similar to what you already know.

Fig. 3.   Social Capital Elements.

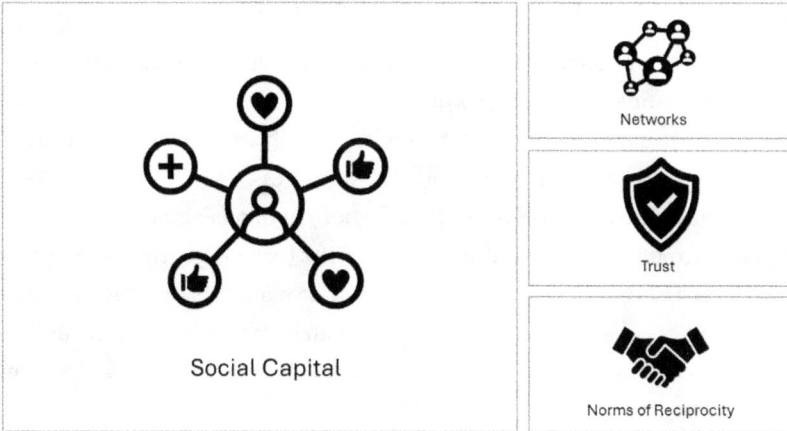

Social Capital

Networks

Trust

Norms of Reciprocity

Source: Adapted from Putnam et al. (1994)

Fig. 4.   Bonding and Bridging Social Capital.

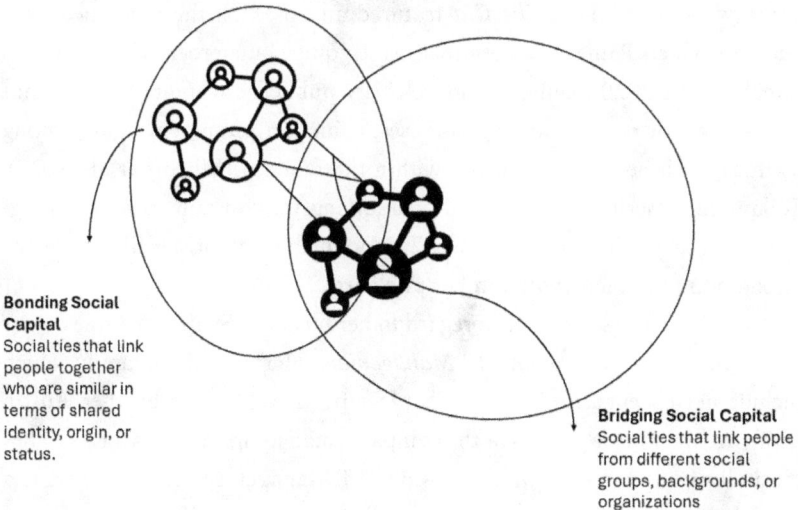

Bonding Social Capital
Social ties that link
people together
who are similar in
terms of shared
identity, origin, or
status.

Bridging Social Capital
Social ties that link people
from different social
groups, backgrounds, or
organizations

Source: Adapted from Putnam et al. (1994).

- *Bridging social capital*: This is the value that comes from more distant connections with people from different social groups. These ties can expose you to new information, resources, and opportunities.

Taylor Swift effectively uses Social Capital Theory in several ways, leveraging her relationships and networks to enhance her career and brand. We will walk through a number of examples and illustrate lessons that other managers and leaders can draw from Swift's success.

Swift has cultivated extensive networks both within her inner circle (bonding social capital) and across different industries (bridging social capital). She has fostered close bonds with her core team of managers, producers, dancers, and other collaborators who work intimately with her. Additionally, her connections across music, fashion, media, and business expose her to new perspectives and opportunities.

Swift has established deep trust with her team by being loyal, valuing their input, and rewarding their hard work. This trust facilitates cooperation and reciprocal support between Swift and those who work for her. Her consistent work ethic and hands-on involvement create norms where her team expects to go above and beyond, strengthening their commitment.

The sheer longevity and dedication of Swift's team members communicate strong network ties and high levels of trust and reciprocity. Trina "Tree" Paine has been Swift's publicist since 2014, committing to taking on Swift as her sole client. *The Cut* featured an op-ed on the renowned publicist, in which Paine was described as a "quiet but ferocious PR pitbull" (Singh-Kurtz, 2020). Unlike many celebrity publicists who are typically not well-known or popular among fanbases, Paine is a prominent figure among Swifties, with her own following within the fandom (Milzoff et al., 2023). Today.com describes Paine as "an unassuming yet constant presence alongside Swift at public events" (Lowe, 2024) which only further illustrates the strong bond between Swift and her publicist.

To keep a close-knit circle in regard to her business, Swift is the sole owner of her management company, *13 Management*. Her immediate family, which include her parents, Andrea and Scott Swift, as well as her brother, Austin Swift, are the top employees at the company, managing various aspects of her music licensing for films and television (13 Management, 2024). Trust is a crucial element in managing a high-profile career like Swift's. By employing family members, Swift ensures that those closest to her have a vested interest in her success and well-being. This level of trust and loyalty is difficult to replicate with non-family members. According to Swift, having her parents, Andrea and Scott Swift, involved in her career decisions has provided her with a reliable support system (Singh-Kurtz, 2020).

Taylor Swift's business relationship with music producer Jack Antonoff is marked by a highly collaborative and creatively synergistic partnership. Jack Antonoff first collaborated with Swift on her 2014 album "1989." This marked the beginning of a productive partnership. Antonoff co-wrote and produced several tracks on the album, including the hit single "Out of the Woods." Their collaboration continued on Swift's subsequent albums, "Reputation" (2017), "Lover" (2019), "Folklore" (2020), "Evermore" (2020), "Midnights" (2022), and most recently "The Tortured Poets Department" (2024).

Antonoff credits Swift with launching his career as a music producer. In an interview with the *New York Times*, Antonoff states that,

> *Taylor's the first person who let me produce a song. Before Taylor, everyone said: 'You're not a producer'. It took Taylor Swift to say: 'I like the way this sounds* (Rosen, 2020).

Like other members of Swift's inner circle, Antonoff is quick to come to Swift's defense. In an interview with the *Los Angeles Times*, Antonoff responded to those who slandered Swift's abilities as a songwriter by stating that questioning her abilities "...is like challenging someone's faith in God. You just don't go there" (Wood, 2024). Antonoff's statements indicate a high level of trust and norm of reciprocity between himself and Swift.

While Swift's core team is tight-knit, she has exposed them to new perspectives through her diverse collaborations and ventures over time. This expands her team's access to novel information, resources, and industry connections, a hallmark of bridging social capital.

Musical collaborations are one of Swift's most notable methods of bridging social capital. Collaborating with other prominent musicians, such as Ed Sheeran, Kendrick Lamar, and Brendon Urie (Dantona, 2023) not only produce hit songs but also expose her to new audiences and strengthen her position within the music industry.

In addition to collaborating with fellow prominent artists, Swift has used her fame to support up-and-coming musicians by featuring them as opening acts on her tours or by collaborating with them on projects. For example, she has promoted artists like Gracie Abrams, Gayle, and Troye Sivan, helping them gain visibility and credibility (Ahlgrim, 2024). These artists, and numerous others, have spoken Swift's praises, further promoting a positive image of her throughout the industry.

Taylor Swift's brand partnerships and endorsements exemplify her strategic use of bridging social capital to expand her reach and influence beyond just the music industry. Swift has collaborated with major brands across various industries like fashion (Keds, Stella McCartney), beverages (Diet Coke, Coca-Cola), cosmetics (CoverGirl), technology (Apple, Sony), finance (Capital One), and retail (Target) (Taylor Swift: Brand Deals, 2024). These partnerships represent bridging social capital by connecting her to new audiences, resources, and perspectives outside her core music fanbase.

By effectively leveraging these relationships and networks, Swift enhances her social capital, which, in turn, contributes to her success and longevity in the highly competitive music industry.

HACKMAN'S FIVE FACTORS OF TEAM EFFECTIVENESS

Renowned psychologist and organizational behavior researcher, Richard Hackman, developed a comprehensive framework to understand what makes teams effective. His 1987 model outlines five key factors that contribute to team effectiveness: a real team, a compelling direction, an enabling structure, a supportive context, and expert coaching (Hackman, 1987, 2002, 2009). Table 4 shows a short description of each factor.

Hackman highlighted that the five key factors are crucial for teams to achieve three important goals: meeting client needs, building skills for future performance, and providing personal satisfaction and growth for team members (Hackman, 2002). According to his model, leaders should focus on creating these five conditions to foster effective teamwork. Ignoring any of these factors can hurt team performance and success (Hackman, 2009).

Because Taylor Swift prefers a close-knit circle and maintains tight control over her business, her operations are more secretive compared to other artists of her caliber (13 Management, 2024). Despite this, we can point to evidence that Taylor Swift works closely with her team members to foster a high-performing and satisfied team.

Swift seems to have assembled a clearly defined, stable team with interdependent members who rely on each other's expertise. Her core team includes her mother Andrea as business manager, longtime publicist Tree Paine, Frank

Table 4. Hackman's Five Factors of Team Effectiveness.

Factors of Team Effectiveness	Description
Real team	The group must be a real team with clear boundaries, stable membership, and interdependence among members to accomplish their work
Compelling direction	The team must have a clear, challenging, and consequential direction that energizes and orients the members toward their mission and goals
Enabling structure	The team's structure, including its composition, norms, and processes, should facilitate effective teamwork and competent performance
Supportive context	The organizational context should provide the necessary resources, rewards, information, and cooperation from other parts of the organization to support the team's work
Expert coaching	Team members should receive expert coaching and guidance to help them develop task strategies, teamwork skills, and overcome obstacles or challenges they face

Source: Summarized from Hackman (1987).

Bell as Director of Radio & Research, Douglas Baldridge as general counsel, and Erica Worden as her personal assistant and road manager (13 Management, 2024; Ian, 2024). This bounded, interdependent group forms a "real team" as per Hackman's model.

Swift provides a clear and compelling direction and vision for her projects, whether it's a new album launch or a world tour. For example, in her seven-week lead up to the launch of the "Midnights" album, Swift used a mix of media channels, award acceptance speeches, film festival appearances, and social media "easter eggs" to entice fans to preorder the upcoming album and related merchandise (Norenius-Raniere, 2024). To accomplish such feats, she must communicate her artistic and business goals effectively for her team to align their efforts with her vision. The goals set by Swift are ambitious yet attainable, providing her team with direction and motivation. Her hands-on approach and emotional investment in her work likely translate into a motivating mission for the team (Kwan, 2024).

Swift's team structure seems enabling, with each member having defined roles (e.g., Paine as publicist, Worden as assistant and road manager, etc.) that facilitate teamwork. Additionally, Swift is described as creating an environment where team members can provide input, with her willingness to hire skilled experts and consider ideas beyond her own (Ian, 2024). "Behind her chart-topping albums and sold-out tours lies a meticulously crafted strategy executed by a team of brilliant minds. From managers to agents, publicists to lawyers, Swift's success story is as much about her talent as it is about the strategic prowess of her business team" (Ian, 2024).

The organization and resources around Swift provide a supportive context. Her ownership of her master recordings and formation of her own management company (Srinivasan, 2023) gives her team autonomy and control. Her massive success and brand power also likely ensure her team has ample organizational support and resources.

Taylor Swift has demonstrated her commitment to mentoring and coaching in various ways throughout her career. For instance, she has served as a "Mega Mentor" on NBC's "The Voice," offering guidance and support to contestants during critical knockout rounds. This role involves helping aspiring artists refine their performances and navigate the complexities of the music industry, showcasing Swift's dedication to nurturing new talent (Rosa, 2023).

Moreover, Swift's approach to mentoring is marked by her genuine care and investment in the growth of others. Kelly Clarkson, a coach on "The Voice," praised Swift for her authentic engagement and dedication to helping contestants, highlighting how she deeply cares about the artists she mentors and actively invests in their development (Rosa, 2023).

These examples reflect Swift's broader philosophy of mentorship, which extends beyond formal roles. She often shares insights from her own experiences, providing valuable lessons and encouragement to both her team and emerging artists. By fostering a supportive environment and demonstrating a commitment to the success of others, Swift exemplifies the principles of effective mentoring and coaching in the music industry.

CONCLUSION

Utilizing the principles of social capital theory and the team effectiveness model, this chapter highlights Swift's strategic approach to surrounding herself with talented professionals, fostering deep trust and reciprocity, and building robust networks that span both close-knit and diverse connections. This chapter explored several ideas, including:

- Leveraging social capital for success by investing time and effort in building strong, trustworthy relationships both within the organization and with external stakeholders.

- Establishing a clear and compelling vision for a business effectively ensures that all team members are aligned and motivated, which are critical aspects for driving performance and achieving business objectives.

- Ensuring that team members have access to the resources they need, are provided regular coaching and feedback, and enjoy a culture of recognition and support not only enhances team performance but also increases job satisfaction and retention.

Aspiring leaders and managers can draw valuable lessons from Swift's methods, applying these insights to build and manage their own high-performing teams.

REFERENCES

13 Management. (2024). *Taylor Swift Switzerland*. https://taylorswiftswitzerland.ch/index.php/wiki/13-management/

Ahlgrim, C. (2024). How Taylor Swift inspired a new generation of singer-songwriters, in their own words. *Business Insider*. https://www.businessinsider.com/artists-inspired-by-taylor-swift-quotes-2022-3

Coffé, H., & Geys, B. (2007). Toward an empirical characterization of bridging and bonding social capital. *Nonprofit and Voluntary Sector Quarterly*, *36*(1), 121–139.

Dantona, S. (2023). Taylor Swift's greatest collaborations: 8 unforgettable duets. *American Songwriter*. https://americansongwriter.com/taylor-swifts-greatest-collaborations-8-unforgettable-duets/

Hackman, J. R. (1987). The design of work groups. In J. W. Lorsch (Ed.), *The handbook of organizational behavior* (pp. 315–342). Prentice-Hall.

Hackman, J. R. (2002). *Leading teams: Setting the stage for great performances.* Harvard Business School Press.

Hackman, J. R. (2009). Why teams don't work. In J. Henry (Ed.), *Creative management and development* (3rd ed.). Sage Publications.

Ian. (2024). *Taylor Swift's business team: Meet the minds behind her success.* Pressfarm. https://press.farm/taylor-swifts-business-team-behind-her-success/

Kwan, K. (2024). *Swift leadership: 6 business lessons from Taylor Swift's chart-topping career.* LinkedIn. https://www.linkedin.com/pulse/swift-leadership-6-business-lessons-from-taylor-yrjuc/

Leana, C. R., & Buren, H. J. (1999). Organizational social capital and employment practices. *The Academy of Management Review, 24*(3), 538–555.

Lowe, L. (2024). Who is Tree Paine? Everything to know about Taylor Swift's powerhouse publicist. *Today.com.* https://www.today.com/popculture/who-is-tree-paine-taylor-swift-rcna148403

Milzoff, R., Renner Brown, E., & Denis, K. (2023). Taylor Swift and Beyoncé are so big, even their publicists have fans. *Billboard.* https://www.billboard.com/business/business-news/taylor-swift-beyonce-publicist-1235398097/

Norenius-Raniere, S. (2024). *Communication lessons from Taylor Swift: Master of the product launch.* Cision. https://www.cision.com/resources/articles/pr-lessons-from-taylor-swift-master-of-the-product-launch/

Obstfeld, D. (2023). Higher aims fulfilled: The Social Capital Academy as a means for advancing underrepresented students in comprehensive university business schools. *Business Horizons, 66*(5), 631–642.

Putnam, R. D., Leonardi, R., & Nanetti, R. Y. (1994). *Making democracy work: Civic traditions in modern Italy.* Princeton University Press.

Rosa, C. (2023). Kelly Clarkson hugged a crying Taylor Swift after the most moving performance. *NBC.com.* Retrieved, 2024, from https://www.nbc.com/nbc-insider/kelly-clarkson-hugged-a-crying-taylor-swift-after-the-most-moving-performance

Rosen, J. (2020). Jack Antonoff is only making music with friends. *New York Times.* https://www.nytimes.com/interactive/2020/03/11/magazine/jack-antonoff-profile.html

Singh-Kurtz, S. (2020). The infamous publicist behind the Taylor Swift machine. *The Cut.* https://www.thecut.com/2020/02/who-is-tree-paine-meet-taylor-swifts-publicist-in-miss-americana.html

Srinivasan, H. (2023). *Taylor Swift's net worth and business empire explained.* Investopedia. https://www.investopedia.com/taylor-swift-earnings-7373918

Swift, T. (2017). *Reputation* [Album]. Big Machine Records.

Swift, T. (2019). *Lover* [Album]. Republic Records.

Swift, T. (2020a). *Folklore* [Album]. Republic Records.

Swift, T. (2020b). *Evermore* [Album]. Republic Records.

Swift, T. (2022). *Midnights* [Album]. Republic Records.

Swift, T. (2024). *The Tortured Poets Department* [Album]. Republic Records.

Taylor Swift: Brand deals. (2024). Taylor Swift Switzerland. https://tay
lorswiftswitzerland.ch/index.php/wiki/brand-deals/

8

OUT OF THE WOODS[1]

ABSTRACT

This chapter examines Taylor Swift's strategic response to losing control over her master recordings, showcasing exemplary crisis management. Swift's decision to re-record her albums illustrates how proactive crisis handling can transform challenges into opportunities. This chapter uses the five phases of crisis management and positive psychological capital to analyze Swift's approach, highlighting her resilience, optimism, and strategic thinking. By navigating adversity and advocating for artist rights, Swift demonstrates effective leadership and the power of taking control of one's destiny.

Keywords: Crisis management; crisis management strategies; positive psychological capital; leadership in adversity; Taylor Swift crisis management

In the fast-paced and often unpredictable worlds of music and business, artists and leaders frequently encounter situations that test their resilience and ingenuity. One such example is Taylor Swift's response to losing control over her master recordings. This chapter delves into how Swift's strategic decision to re-record her previous albums serves as an exemplary case of

---

[1]Swift, T. (2021). Out of the Woods [Song]. *On 1989* (Taylor's Version). Republic Records.

crisis management. Faced with the adversity of her master recordings being acquired by an entity she did not trust, Swift's proactive approach not only safeguarded her brand and financial interests but also transformed a challenging situation into a powerful opportunity for growth and empowerment (Grinstein & Kronzon, 2020).

The title "Out of the Woods" reflects the journey Swift undertook to navigate and ultimately emerge from a complex and challenging situation. Swift's handling of this crisis can be thoroughly understood through the lens of the five phases of crisis management: signal detection, preparation/prevention, damage containment, recovery, and learning. Each phase reveals the depth of her strategic thinking and the meticulous planning that underpinned her actions. Additionally, this analysis incorporates the concept of positive psychological capital, highlighting how Swift's optimism, resilience, and confidence played a critical role in navigating the crisis and emerging stronger.

By examining Swift's journey through these phases, this chapter aims to provide a comprehensive understanding of effective crisis management. It offers valuable insights not only for artists and industry professionals but also for anyone looking to learn from Swift's exemplary leadership and crisis-handling capabilities. Through her story, we explore how adversity can be transformed into an opportunity for reinvention and how taking charge of one's destiny can lead to remarkable outcomes.

THE FIVE PHASES OF CRISIS MANAGEMENT

An *organizational crisis* is a rare but high-impact event that threatens the organization's survival. It often involves unclear causes, effects, and solutions and creates a sense of urgency for quick decision-making (Pearson & Clair, 1998). Crisis management is effective when the organization can continue or restart essential operations, maintaining the necessary momentum to meet key customer needs. It also involves minimizing losses for both the organization and external stakeholders and ensuring that lessons learned are applied to future incidents (Pearson & Clair, 1998).

A crisis management model serves as a conceptual framework encompassing all stages of preparing for, preventing, responding to, and recovering from a crisis. Utilizing a model allows crisis managers to contextualize events and more effectively implement best practices (Marker, 2020).

Fig. 5.   Five Stage Model for Crisis Management.

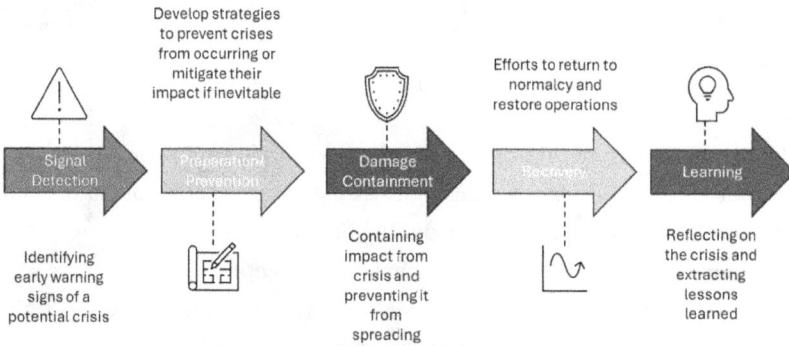

Develop strategies
to prevent crises
from occurring or
mitigate their
impact if inevitable

Efforts to return to
normalcy and
restore operations

Signal
Detection

Preparation/
Prevention

Damage
Containment

Recovery

Learning

Identifying
early warning
signs of a
potential crisis

Containing
impact from
crisis and
preventing it
from
spreacing

Reflecting on
the crisis and
extracting
lessons
learned

Adapted from Pearson and Mitroff Five Stage Model for Crisis Management (Pearson & Mitroff, 1993).

Pearson and Mitroff's (1993) Five Phases of Crisis Management Model is particularly helpful for understanding the stages through which nearly all crises pass through. From early warning signals to prevention, through damage containment and business recovery, to organizational learning, each phase carries its own risks and opportunities. By effectively managing each stage, organizations can enhance their ability to handle crises (Pearson & Mitroff, 1993).

The five phases of crisis management provide a structured framework for understanding and responding to crises. These phases help organizations and individuals to prepare for, navigate through, and learn from crises effectively. The phases are illustrated in Fig. 5.

Phase 1: Signal Detection

In the signal detection phase, organizations identify early warning signs by monitoring their internal and external environments to anticipate potential crises (Pearson & Mitroff, 1993). Key activities include scanning for threats and vulnerabilities, establishing early warning systems, encouraging open communication for reporting concerns, and analyzing data and trends. For example, a technology company might track social media mentions and customer feedback to detect dissatisfaction that could escalate into a public relations issue.

By identifying these signs early, the company can address the root causes before they become larger problems, allowing for timely and proactive responses.

Phase 2: Preparation/Prevention

The preparation/prevention phase involves developing strategies to prevent crises or mitigate their impact through risk assessments, crisis planning, and training (Fearn-Banks, 2016; Pearson & Mitroff, 1993).

Organizations conduct risk assessments to identify potential crisis scenarios, develop crisis management plans and response protocols, and train employees on crisis response procedures. For instance, a hospital might conduct regular emergency drills and develop detailed plans for handling potential health outbreaks. By having these measures in place, the hospital ensures that it can respond effectively and minimize the impact of a crisis when it occurs. Creating communication plans for both internal and external stakeholders is also crucial, ensuring clear and coordinated responses during a crisis.

Phase 3: Damage Containment

Once a crisis hits, the focus shifts to containing its impact and preventing it from spreading in the damage containment phase (Coombs et al., 2019; Pearson & Mitroff, 1993). Quick and decisive action is crucial to manage the immediate effects of the crisis. Key activities include activating crisis management plans, implementing immediate response measures, clear communication with stakeholders, and managing media relations. For example, a food company facing a product contamination issue might recall the affected products, issue public apologies, and provide regular updates on the situation. These actions help limit the damage caused by the crisis, maintain organizational stability, and reassure stakeholders that the issue is being handled responsibly.

Phase 4: Recovery

The recovery phase involves efforts to return to normalcy and restore operations after the immediate crisis has been contained (Coombs et al., 2019; Pearson & Mitroff, 1993). This phase focuses on repairing damage, rebuilding trust, and learning from the crisis to improve future resilience. Activities include assessing the damage, implementing recovery plans to restore operations and services, and providing support to affected individuals and stakeholders. For instance, after a natural disaster, a retail company might work to quickly reopen stores, offer assistance to impacted employees, and communicate with customers about recovery efforts. The goal is to recover from the crisis and return to normal operations as quickly and efficiently as possible, ensuring the organization can continue to serve its stakeholders effectively.

Phase 5: Learning

In the learning phase (Pearson & Mitroff, 1993), organizations reflect on the crisis and the response to it, extracting lessons learned and making improvements to prevent future crises. This phase ensures continuous improvement and organizational learning. Key activities include conducting post-crisis evaluations and debriefings, analyzing what worked well and what didn't, updating crisis management plans and protocols, and sharing insights with the broader organization. For example, after handling a data breach, a financial institution might review its response to identify areas for improvement, update its cybersecurity measures, and share lessons learned with other departments. The goal is to enhance organizational resilience and preparedness by learning from the crisis and improving future responses, ensuring the organization is better equipped to handle future challenges.

Pearson and Mitroff's model emphasizes the importance of proactive crisis management, with a focus on early detection, prevention, and learning from past experiences to enhance an organization's crisis preparedness and resilience.

Taylor Swift and her team were forced to go into crisis management mode in 2019 when the battle over her master recordings began. Swift *detected* the potential crisis when her former label Big Machine Records was acquired by Scooter Braun's company in 2019, giving him control over the masters of her first six albums, which she considered her "worst case scenario" (Toia, 2023). In a Tumblr post, Swift expressed her dissatisfaction with the business deal:

> For years I asked, pleaded for a chance to own my work. Instead I
> was given an opportunity to sign back up to Big Machine Records
> and 'earn' one album back at a time, one for every new one I turned
> in. I walked away because I knew once I signed that contract, Scott

> Borchetta (founder of Big Machine Label Group) would sell the
> label, thereby selling me and my future. I had to make the excruciat-
> ing choice to leave behind my past. (Swift, 2019).

Swift and her former recording label, Big Machine Label Group (BMLG) continued battling it out over the rights to Swift's music, both on social media and in the legal system (Meiselman, 2019; Toia, 2023). When it was apparent that the loss of her master recordings was, indeed, inevitable, Swift *prepared* a detailed plan to re-record her albums, a move that would allow her to own the new versions of these songs and regain control over her music. This strategy also involved legal and marketing preparations to ensure the new recordings would be recognized and accepted by her fanbase.

Swift effectively *contained the damage* of losing her masters by communicating her plan to re-record her albums to her fans and the public in August 2019, when she performed in Central Park at Good Morning America, a day prior to the release of the *Lover* album (her first album release under her new label, Republic Records) (Toia, 2023). After her performance, in her interview with Robin Roberts, Swift explained her reasons and the importance of owning her work (Andrews, 2019). This transparency helped to maintain her fan support. By re-recording her albums, she also aimed to direct consumer preference toward her new versions, reducing the value of the originals held by Ithaca Holdings.

Swift's re-recording project can be seen as a *recovery* strategy. By releasing "Taylor's Versions" of her albums, she not only reclaimed her music but also added new value by including previously unreleased tracks. This endeavor allowed her to continue her career on her own terms, reinforcing her autonomy and creative control. She also negotiated to own the masters for all music created from 2019 onward when signing with Republic Records (Grady, 2019).

The final stage involves analyzing the crisis and the response to it, *learning* from it, and improving future crisis management strategies. Swift's experience serves as a lesson for other artists and individuals in similar situations about the importance of understanding contractual rights and taking proactive steps to secure their intellectual property. Swift has also used her platform to advocate for artists' rights, sharing her experience as a cautionary tale and encouraging others to be vigilant and proactive about their own work.

Swift's proactive approach, involving re-recording her albums and negotiating favorable terms with her new label, exemplifies Pearson and Mitroff's crisis management model. Her actions allowed her to regain control, mitigate damage, and drive positive changes in the industry.

POSITIVE PSYCHOLOGICAL CAPITAL

Maintaining a positive psychological mindset, known as psychological capital (PsyCap), is crucial for leaders, especially after facing major crises. PsyCap is a combination of hope, self-efficacy, resilience, and optimism (Luthans et al., 2007). It helps leaders cope better with challenges, bounce back from setbacks, and maintain a positive outlook (Luthans & Youssef-Morgan, 2017).

Positive psychological capital (PsyCap) is a concept within organizational behavior and psychology that focuses on the positive developmental state of an individual. It is composed of four key components, often summarized with the acronym *HERO* (see Fig. 6).

Hope

Hope involves having a goal-oriented mindset and the ability to generate multiple pathways to achieve these goals, along with the motivation to

Fig. 6.   Positive Psychological Capital.

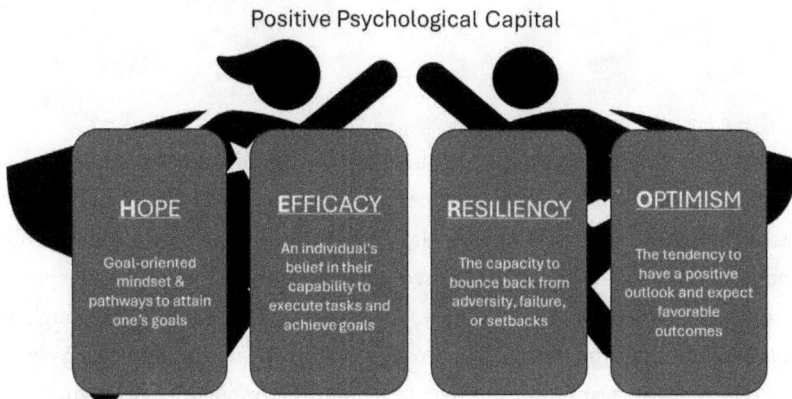

Positive Psychological Capital

HOPE — Goal-oriented mindset & pathways to attain one's goals

EFFICACY — An individual's belief in their capability to execute tasks and achieve goals

RESILIENCY — The capacity to bounce back from adversity, failure, or setbacks

OPTIMISM — The tendency to have a positive outlook and expect favorable outcomes

Adapted from Luthans et al. (2007).

pursue them (Luthans & Jensen, 2002; Snyder et al., 1991). Effective leaders utilize hope by setting clear and attainable goals for themselves and their teams. For example, a project manager might outline several strategies to meet a tight deadline and motivate the team to explore different approaches until they find the most efficient one. By fostering a hopeful environment, leaders encourage persistence and resilience among team members, enabling them to overcome obstacles and continue working toward their objectives even when faced with challenges.

Efficacy (Self-efficacy)

Efficacy refers to an individual's belief in their capability to execute tasks and achieve goals (Bandura, 1997). It is the confidence in one's abilities to take on and successfully perform specific tasks. Effective leaders can boost their team's self-efficacy by providing constructive feedback, recognizing achievements, and offering opportunities for skill development. For instance, a sales manager might coach a new salesperson, helping them build confidence through small wins and gradually increasing their responsibilities. High self-efficacy leads to greater effort and perseverance in challenging situations, as individuals believe in their competence to handle tasks and solve problems, ultimately driving higher performance (Stajkovic & Luthans, 1998).

Resilience

Resilience is the capacity to bounce back from adversity, failure, or setbacks (Luthans et al., 2006). It involves maintaining or quickly regaining mental health and well-being despite difficulties. Effective leaders demonstrate resilience by remaining calm and composed during crises, providing a stable presence for their teams. For example, a CEO navigating a company through a financial downturn might openly communicate the challenges, outline a clear recovery plan, and support employees through the transition. Resilient leaders inspire their teams to cope with stress, recover from disappointments, and adapt to changing circumstances, enabling the organization to move forward and thrive despite setbacks (Youssef & Luthans, 2007).

Optimism

Optimism is the tendency to have a positive outlook and expect favorable outcomes (Seligman, 1998). It involves attributing positive events to internal, stable, and global causes while viewing negative events as external, temporary, and situation-specific. Effective leaders harness optimism by maintaining a positive attitude, even in difficult times, and encouraging their teams to do the same. For instance, a department head facing a tough project might highlight past successes and emphasize the team's strengths, fostering a belief that they can achieve their goals. Optimistic leaders enhance motivation, reduce stress, and improve overall performance and satisfaction, creating a more productive and positive work environment (Luthans et al., 2007).

By cultivating PsyCap, leaders can navigate crises more effectively, overcome anxiety and stress, and ensure that individuals and organizations function at their best (Avey et al., 2009). Additionally, PsyCap has been shown to improve mental health, emotional well-being, and overall psychological functioning (Avey et al., 2010), which are essential for leaders under immense pressure during crises.

Importantly, PsyCap promotes teamwork, cooperation, and a sense of unity among employees (Luthans et al., 2008), which are vital for organizational recovery and adaptation after a crisis. Furthermore, leaders with high PsyCap can inspire and motivate their teams through their hopefulness, optimism, and resilience, creating a positive work environment that fosters overcoming challenges and future growth (Luthans & Youssef-Morgan, 2017).

Throughout the crisis surrounding the acquisition of her master recordings, Taylor Swift demonstrated the key elements of positive psychological capital – hope, efficacy, resilience, and optimism.

Swift maintained *hope* that she could regain control over her artistic works by announcing her intention to re-record her entire catalog. Swift aimed to regain control over her music by re-recording her old albums. This clear objective gave her a focused direction amidst the crisis. She explored and executed the strategy of creating "Taylor's Versions" of her albums. This creative and legal pathway allowed her to circumvent the restrictions posed by the ownership of her original masters (Humayun, 2023).

Taylor Swift showed high self-*efficacy* by her confidence in her capacity to re-record her albums successfully even though it required revisiting and perfecting work from earlier in her career. Her confidence in her artistic capabilities empowered her to take on this unconventional approach.

Faced with the significant setback of losing control over her master recordings, Swift didn't succumb to defeat. Instead, she bounced back by finding a proactive solution through re-recording her music. Swift displayed remarkable *resilience* by continuing to produce critically acclaimed albums like "Folklore," "Evermore," and "Midnights" amidst working on her re-recording project (Le, 2020). Her resilience allowed her to maintain her creative momentum and productivity during the crisis.

Throughout the crisis, Swift maintained a positive attitude, focusing on the opportunity to reassert control over her music rather than dwelling on the negative aspects of losing her masters. Swift's public statements and actions reflected an *optimistic* outlook, as she firmly believed in the importance of artists owning their work and advocated for systemic changes in the industry (Perton, 2024). Swift's belief in the success of her "Taylor's Versions" reflected her optimistic mindset. Her confidence that fans would support and prefer her re-recordings over the originals showed her expectation of favorable outcomes. Her optimism inspired positive changes and influenced record labels to adjust their practices.

By drawing upon the elements of hope, efficacy, resilience, and optimism, Swift navigated the crisis surrounding her master recordings with positive psychological capital. Her proactive approach, unwavering creativity, and advocacy for artists' rights exemplified the power of a positive mindset in overcoming adversity.

CONCLUSION

Taylor Swift's strategic response to the crisis of losing control over her master recordings exemplifies effective crisis management and the power of positive psychological capital. This chapter has explored how Swift's proactive decision to re-record her albums safeguarded her brand and financial interests while transforming a significant challenge into an opportunity for growth and empowerment.

Throughout this chapter, we explored the following concepts:

- Being proactive when it comes to crises allows individuals and organizations to address issues before they escalate, minimizing potential damage and maintaining stability.

- Cultivating positive psychological capital within leadership and the broader organization can enhance resilience and improve outcomes during crises.

- Leaders should prioritize transparent and effective communication with all stakeholders during crises. By being open about the challenges faced and the steps being taken to address them, leaders and organizations can maintain trust, garner support, and navigate through difficult times more effectively.

Swift's journey offers valuable insights for leaders in any field. Her story underscores how adversity can be transformed into an opportunity for reinvention and how taking proactive control of one's destiny can lead to remarkable outcomes. Through her actions, Swift not only reclaimed her music but also advocated for broader changes within the industry, demonstrating the far-reaching impact of effective crisis management and positive psychological capital.

REFERENCES

Andrews, T. (2019). Analysis | Can Taylor Swift really rerecord her entire music catalogue? *The Washington Post.* https://www.washingtonpost.com/arts-entertainment/2019/08/22/can-taylor-swift-really-rerecord-her-entire-music-catalogue/

Avey, J. B., Luthans, F., & Jensen, S. M. (2009). Psychological capital: A positive resource for combating employee stress and turnover. *Human Resource Management, 48*(5), 677–693.

Avey, J. B., Luthans, F., Smith, R. M., & Palmer, N. F. (2010). Impact of positive psychological capital on employee well-being over time. *Journal of Occupational Health Psychology, 15*(1), 17–28.

Bandura, A. (1997). *Self-efficacy: The exercise of control.* W.H. Freeman and Company.

Coombs, W. T., Holladay, S. J., & Tachkova, E. (2019). Crisis communication, risk communication, and issues management. In B. R. Brunner (Ed.), *Public relations theory: Application and understanding* (pp. 31–48). Wiley Blackwell.

Fearn-Banks, K. (2016). *Crisis communications: A casebook approach* (5th ed.). Routledge.

Grady, C. (2019). Why Taylor Swift is rerecording all her old songs. *Vox.* https://www.vox.com/culture/22278732/taylor-swift-re-recording-1989-speak-now-enchanted-mine-master-rights-scooter-braun

Grinstein, Y., & Kronzon, S. (2020). *The power of resilience: How successful leaders thrive in times of adversity*. Harvard Business Review Press.

Humayun, H. (2023). *The legal harmony: Taylor Swift's re-recording saga and its implications*. LinkedIn. https://www.linkedin.com/pulse/legal-harmony-taylor-swifts-re-recording-saga-its-haris-humayun/

Le, C. (2020). Column: Taylor Swift's resilience can inspire all. *Daily Titan*. https://dailytitan.com/opinion/column-taylor-swifts-resilience-can-inspire-all/article_70cb6ea2-4008-11eb-a86f-07cc124abcd7.html

Luthans, F., Avolio, B. J., Avey, J. B., & Norman, S. M. (2007). Positive psychological capital: Measurement and relationship with performance and satisfaction. *Personnel Psychology*, 60(3), 541–572. https://doi.org/10.1111/j.1744-6570.2007.00083.x

Luthans, F., & Jensen, S. M. (2002). Hope: A new positive strength for human resource development. *Human Resource Development Review*, 1(3), 304–322. https://doi.org/10.1177

Luthans, F., Norman, S. M., Avolio, B. J., & Avey, J. B. (2008). The mediating role of psychological capital in the supportive organizational climate—employee performance relationship. *Journal of Organizational Behavior: The International Journal of Industrial, Occupational and Organizational Psychology and Behavior*, 29(2), 219–238.

Luthans, F., Vogelgesang, G. R., & Lester, P. B. (2006). Developing the psychological capital of resiliency. *Human Resource Development Review*, 5(1), 25–44. https://doi.org/10.1177/1534484305285335

Luthans, F., Youssef, C. M., & Avolio, B. J. (2007). *Psychological capital: Developing the human competitive edge*. Oxford University Press.

Luthans, F., & Youssef-Morgan, C. M. (2017). Psychological capital: An evidence-based positive approach. *Annual Review of Organizational Psychology and Organizational Behavior*, 4(1), 339–366.

Marker, A. (2020). *Crisis management models & theories L Smartsheet*. Smartsheet. https://www.smartsheet.com/content/crisis-management-model-theories

Meiselman, J. (2019) Taylor Swift's messy legal situation, Explained. *VICE*. https://www.vice.com/en/article/wjw3v4/taylor-swifts-messy-legal-situation-with-scooter-braun-big-machine-explained

Pearson, C. M., & Clair, J. A. (1998). Reframing crisis management. *Academy of Management Review*, 23(1), 59–76.

Pearson, C. M., & Mitroff, I. I. (1993). From crisis prone to crisis prepared: A framework for crisis management. *The Executive*, 7(1), 48–59. http://www.jstor.org/stable/4165107

Perton, V. (2024). *Taylor Swift: Magnetic optimism and joy*. The Centre for Optimism. https://www.centreforoptimism.com/blog/taylor-swift-magnetic-optimism-and-joy

Seligman, M. E. P. (1998). *Learned optimism: How to change your mind and your life*. Pocket Books.

Snyder, C. R., Irving, L., & Anderson, J. R. (1991). Hope and health: Measuring the will and the ways. In C. R. Snyder & D. R. Forsyth (Eds.), *Handbook of social and clinical psychology: The health perspective* (pp. 285–305). Pergamon Press.

Stajkovic, A. D., & Luthans, F. (1998). Self-efficacy and work-related performance: A meta-analysis. *Psychological Bulletin, 124*(2), 240–261. https://doi.org/10.1037

Swift, T. (2019). *For years I asked, pleaded for a chance to own my…* Taylor Swift. https://taylorswift.tumblr.com/post/185958366550/for-years-i-asked-pleaded-for-a-chance-to-own-my.

Swift, T. (2019, June 30). *For years I asked, pleaded for a chance to own my work*. Tumblr. https://taylorswift.tumblr.com/post/185958366550/for-years-i-asked-pleaded-for-a-chance-to-own-my

Toia, L. (2023). *Taylor Swift's legal battle for the ownership of her master recordings: A music copyright debacle that illustrates the power of social media amidst legal proceedings*. LINDSAY TOIA. https://www.lindsaytoia.com/blog/taylor-swifts-legal-battle-for-the-ownership-of-her-master-recordings

Youssef, C. M., & Luthans, F. (2007). Positive organizational behavior in the workplace: The impact of hope, optimism, and resilience. *Journal of Management, 33*(5), 774–800. https://doi.org/10.1177/0149206307305562

9

ANTI-HERO[1]

ABSTRACT

Taylor Swift has shown herself to be an effective leader who influences many people. However, like all leaders, there are some flaws and challenges with her leadership. This chapter explores several of those. It first considers some of the positives of looking up to leaders as heroes before suggesting some negatives of hero worship. The chapter then advocates the importance of considering context when modeling the behavior of other leaders. It concludes by specifically addressing a few criticisms of Swift's leadership and influence including: the use of her private jet, her involvement in politics, her potential overselling to fans, and her status as a role model to younger fans.

Keywords: Heroes; criticisms; role models; celebrity; Taylor Swift leadership

This book has explored the leadership style and behaviors of Taylor Swift. Largely, it has assumed that Swift's leadership has been effective, moral, positive, and generally "good." However, there can be a danger in "hero worship" when analyzing the leadership of one specific leader.

---

[1]Swift, T. (2022). Anti-Hero [Song]. On *Midnights*. Republic Records.

In the song "Anti-Hero," Swift reflects on challenges and shortcomings. At one point, she suggests that she has some flaws to the point where she labels herself as problematic. Some critics have suggested that one of the messages behind the song is to caution listeners not to place celebrities (such as Swift herself) on a pedestal (Uitti, 2022).

HERO WORSHIP

This chapter explores the dangers of such "hero worship" including considering the potential problems of emulating celebrities (such as, but not limited to Swift) in one's own leadership roles. It will conclude by providing a few examples where Swift herself may have made some missteps in her leadership, furthermore providing evidence for the dangers of relying too much on celebrities for learning about leadership.

Potential Dangers of Hero Worship

Hero worship occurs when people place others on a pedestal and idolize them. On the one hand, having heroes and looking up to them can provide some benefits. Looking up to heroes can provide role models to emulate, helps to elevate positive emotions, and can lead to psychological growth (Allison & Goethals, 2016).

Sometimes, the people placed on pedestals are very public figures. They can be celebrities or publicly visible leaders, for example. In the case of Taylor Swift, she is both a celebrity and visible leader and, as such, can sometimes experience hero worship from her fans who think that she can do no wrong. Looking up to heroes (or celebrities) too much to the point of where they are idolized can be detrimental. For example, studies have shown that doing so can negatively impact a follower's (or fan's) mental health (Maltby et al., 2004). When people begin to worship their heroes, leaders, or celebrities, they tend to overlook the mistakes that their heroes can make. In other words, they view these individuals to be somewhat infallible or perfect.

The problem, of course, is that most (if not all) leaders actually do wrong from time to time. They may not do it purposefully, but all leaders make mistakes. So, placing leaders on a pedestal is not ideal (Urick, 2022) because they are not perfect.

Considering a leader to be infallible is greatly problematic because they hold a lot of influence over followers. If a leader is not ever questioned because they are viewed to always be right or even perfect, then followers could be led down a path that they would not go otherwise.

Of course, in Taylor Swift's case, we have been suggesting throughout this book that she engages in a number of positive behaviors. We are not changing our minds in this late chapter by saying that she could lead followers down an immoral path. However, we are suggesting that she is not perfect and imperfections of any leader should be understood because it is important to always question leaders to ensure that they align with our own ideals. A few examples of Swift's potential missteps that relate to her leadership will be noted later in this chapter. But, before turning to that, we also should consider one specific challenge of emulating a celebrity-leader too much and the challenge is that context matters.

Problems from Emulating Celebrities

There are many problems with looking at celebrities and emulating their leadership style. First, of course, is that some celebrities may make poor decisions. Or, potentially even worse, they may be immoral. Though Swift has made some potential missteps as we will note below, we have spent the majority of this book suggesting that Swift is a good leader, so we will assume in this section that the dangers of emulating her leadership style are not related to poor choices or morality.

Instead, one pitfall of emulating Swift (and other celebrities) is that her context is not like ours. It is not likely that many of us will be multi-platinum global pop music stars. Nor are many of us born with the natural talent toward songwriting in the same way as Swift. So, our contexts are different.

By context, we mean a variety of things all related to one's environment in which they operate. For example, not all leaders will have the same followers. Followers will differ based on the types of goals that leaders seek to influence them to accomplish. For example, followers will differ based on their readiness (Simmons & Hoidn, 2023). Readiness is concerned with how able and willing followers are to accomplish a task.

Swift has two groups of followers: one group are the people that she works with professionally such as producers, venue staff, musicians, and others that she relies on to put out her primary products of live and recorded music. The second group of followers that she influences are her fans. While we will all have cow-orkers and followers similar to that first group that Swift influences, it is unlikely that we will have millions of world-wide adoring fans speculating about every move that we make that we seek to influence whether through our message or just to purchase our songs and albums. Therefore, much of how a leader seeks to influence will depend on attributes of their followers and, because most of us are not celebrities, we likely will not have fans that we must influence.

Another aspect of what varies from celebrities to our own situations is the cultures in which they operate. Every culture is unique, and each leader oper-ates within a culture. In fact, every social group has its own culture that is comprised of assumptions (those unspoken rules or ways of thinking), values (those things that people care about), and artifacts (the physical manifesta-tions of culture that encompass the things we can see, hear, touch, smell, and/or even taste; Schein, 2010).

The cultures that Swift works in are not the same as the cultures in which we lead. For example, Swift's fans have their own culture. While some ele-ments of their culture may be similar to our own organizations' (such as valuing respect for others), the artifacts (such as bead bracelets traded at concerts) are likely vastly different. The point here is that leaders must under-stand the cultures in which they operate to effectively lead it. Because our cultures are not exactly like Swift's, it suggests that we are not simply able to mimic her leadership styles and behaviors exactly.

This is not to say that learning about the leadership styles of others, includ-ing Swift, is not valuable. We can always learn from others. But, it is important to understand the theories that can explain what makes a particular leader effective in their own context so that we can best understand how that theory can be applied to our unique situations. That is why, in every chapter, we've linked Swift's leadership to academically supported leadership theories. This is so readers can understand the theories through examples from Swift so that they might better understand how they apply to their own contexts.

POTENTIAL MISSTEPS IN SWIFT'S LEADERSHIP

And, of course, Taylor Swift is not perfect. So those that follow her or would like to emulate her leadership style must look at it with a critical eye as they should of all leaders. Of course, there are some criticisms about Swift out there fueled by misogyny, conspiracy theories, or sheer jealousy. This section attempts to steer clear of those to focus on three criticisms that are more valid.

The first is related to Swift's travel, specifically on her private jet. In a high-profile 2024 trip to see Travis Kelce play in the Super Bowl, Swift traveled in her private jet from Japan to the USA (Thorbecke, 2024). Critics have suggested that this can do quite a bit of damage to the planet as the emissions from one person flying on a private plane for personal purposes are harmful to the environment. As someone who sets an example to others, critics have argued that Swift's use of her private plane suggests that it is okay to harm the environment for personal reasons (Larson, 2022). Though Swift has purchased carbon credits to try and offset these emissions (the effectiveness of which is also often called into question), other artists such as Coldplay and Billie Eilish have made more of an effort of integrating sustainability initiatives into their tours (Mendez, 2024).

Others have criticized Swift for her role in politics. While some have argued that Swift has been involved in the politics of the USA, others suggest that she has not been strong enough in talking about issues important to her (Nardino, 2023). These critics suggest that Swift could use her leadership to influence government leaders to create policies to benefit the marginalized who may not possess as much power as Swift to speak out for themselves.

Additionally, Swift has been criticized for being overly influential to her followers by manipulating her fans to pay for multiple versions of her albums to hear bonus tracks available exclusively only via certain vendors (n.a., 2023). For example, for her "1989" album, she released a vinyl version featuring exclusive songs and album artwork for only 48 hours. But, once the 48 hours were up, she released another exclusive version with different artwork and exclusive songs that would again only be available for 48 hours (Shafer, 2023). This is but one example of fans needing to spend considerable amounts of money in order to hear all of Swift's songs (she repeated a similar approach again for her latest album, "The Tortured Poets Department") (Swift, 2024).

This could be perceived as taking advantage of some of her most devoted fans, which could negatively impact trust between her and her followers over time.

Swift has also been criticized recently for the content of her most recent album at the time of writing, "The Tortured Poets Department" (Hanawalt, 2024). Over the course of her career, Swift has become an inspiration for children, especially young women, who look up to her. A quick search on Amazon shows that there are several children's books about her. Some critics have found her later lyrics, especially those on "The Tortured Poets Department" to be inappropriate for children, many of whom idolize her, buy her albums, attend her concerts, and are ultimately influenced by her. Some parents have found that, while they might themselves enjoy the album, Swift's use of swear words, themes of death and killing, mentions of substance use, and sexual references to be too mature for their kids (Hanawalt, 2024). Certainly, Swift and other artists should be able to grow and mature, and this should be reflected in their lyrics. But, for Swift who we have argued to be a leader throughout this book, there is a specific challenge to not alienate some of her most devoted followers with more mature content. Furthermore, there may also be a level of responsibility that leaders may need to take with regard to how they influence followers. The implication for Swift is a question of whether she has a responsibility to her younger listeners/followers/fans to emphasize themes that would be more appropriate for their age demographic.

With each of these examples (and others not explicitly addressed here), we must ask ourselves whether Swift is ethical in her decisions and use of influence. Our purpose is not to suggest that she is ethical or unethical – instead, it is to suggest that all followers must question leaders. And all aspiring leaders must come to know their own values as they model their own leadership with the leadership styles of others.

CONCLUSION

As with all celebrities and all leaders, we should be cautious to put Taylor Swift on a pedestal and consider her leadership to be perfect.

- To consider a leader to be infallible suggests that we are engaging in hero worship. We should avoid doing this with leaders because every leader makes mistakes. No leader is perfect. And so, as we seek to learn from leaders, we should always question their limitations.

- One issue of modeling our own leadership with that of others including celebrities is that their context is different. Swift's leadership reality is different from our own because she has a different context. The nature of her followers and culture of the social groups in which she operates are likely very different than those in which we operate. Therefore, we should not blindly model our own leadership after hers without taking the context into consideration.

- Swift, like all leaders, is not without some valid criticism in her leadership. In the case of Swift, some of this criticism is related to the ethics behind some of her decisions. As we seek to improve our own leadership effectiveness, it is important to reflect on the ethics of the leaders we seek to emulate as well as our own ethical decisions that we make.

Again, though we have noted some pitfalls of modeling leadership styles with Swift's, we would like to reiterate that she has done a lot of good with the decisions that she has made and the influence that she has wielded. The following concluding chapter summarizes these decisions and modes of influence that we have explored throughout the book.

REFERENCES

Allison, S. T., & Goethals, G. R. (2016). Hero worship: The elevation of the human spirit. *Journal for the Theory of Social Behaviour*, 46(2), 187–210.

Hanawalt, Z. (2024, April 19). *Taylor Swift's 'The Tortured Poets Department' dropped, but is it appropriate for tweens?*. Parents. Retrieved July 2, 2024, from https://www.parents.com/is-taylor-swifts-new-album-appropriate-for-tweens-8636280

Larson, S. (2022, July 29). Taylor Swift's private jet usage sparks backlash amid climate crisis. *The Guardian*. https://www.theguardian.com/environment/2022/jul/29/taylor-swift-private-jet-usage-climate-crisis

Maltby, J., Day, L., McCutcheon, L. E., Gillett, R., Houran, J., & Ashe, D. D. (2004). Personality and coping: A context for examining celebrity worship and mental health. *British Journal of Psychology*, 95(4), 411–428.

Mendez, L. (2024, February 13). Taylor Swift claims she offsets her carbon footprint – How does that work?. *BBC*. Retrieved June 24, 2024, from https://www.bbc.com/travel/article/20240213-taylor-swift-private-jet-flight-travel-carbon-footprint

n.a. (2023, August 22). Taylor Swift's dedicated fans have accused her of being "Shameless" for trying to "Exploit" them with "Money Grabbing" tactics. *Buzzfeed*.

Nardino, M. (2023, July 28). Taylor Swift's biggest controversies through the years: From feuding with Kanye West to copyright lawsuits. *US Magazine*.

Schein, E. H. (2010). *Organizational culture and leadership*. John Wiley & Sons.

Simmons, E., & Hoidn, S. (2023). *Situational leadership*. Sage Knowledge. Retrieved February 25, 2024, from https://sk.sagepub.com/foundations/situational-leadership

Thorbecke, C. (2024, February 6). Taylor Swift threatens legal action against Florida student who tracks her jet. *CNN*.

Uitti, J. (2022, October 27). Go behind the meaning of the New Taylor Swift Single, 'Anti-Hero'. *American Songwriter*. Retrieved January 5, 2024.

Urick, M. J. (2022). *Leadership in multigenerational organizations: Strategies to successfully manage an age diverse workforce*. Emerald Publishing Limited. https://doi.org/10.1108/978-1-83982-734-120221013

Shafer, E. (2023, August 18). Taylor Swift unveils limited-edition yellow vinyl of "1989 (Taylor's Version)" for 48 hours. *Billboard*. https://www.billboard.com/music/music-news/taylor-swift-1989-taylors-version-limited-edition-yellow-vinyl-1235394784/

Swift, T. (2024). *The Tortured Poets Department* [Album]. Republic Records.

10

ALL TOO WELL[1]

ABSTRACT

This final chapter encapsulates the key moments and leadership lessons from Taylor Swift's career. Throughout the book, we've seen Swift's visionary leadership, creativity, resilience, and authenticity. By exploring her strategic decisions and transformative leadership style, we offer aspiring leaders actionable insights on setting clear goals, motivating others, embracing innovation, and leading with integrity. As we conclude, we shift from reflection to action, encouraging readers to apply these principles in their own leadership journeys.

Keywords: Taylor Swift leadership; visionary leadership; creativity in leadership; resilient leadership; authentic leadership

As we wrap up our look at Taylor Swift's incredible journey, it's clear her story is about more than just music. Taylor Swift's rise to fame is packed with lessons on leadership, influence, and being true to yourself. This book has explored various parts of her career to uncover the strategies that have made her a top figure in the music industry and beyond. This final chapter, titled "All Too Well," sums up the key moments and lessons from Swift's career, much like the song captures her artistic and personal growth.

---

[1] Swift, T. (2021). All Too Well [Song]. *On Red* (Taylor's Version). Republic Records.

Throughout the book, we saw how Swift's leadership shines in different ways. In "Wildest Dreams,"[2] we learned about having a clear vision and setting big goals, inspired by Swift's early career dreams. "Fearless"[3] showed us the power of transformational leadership and how Swift motivates and inspires others with her authenticity and determination.

"Sparks Fly"[4] focused on creativity and innovation, highlighting Swift's ability to push boundaries and stay fresh. "Enchanted"[5] looked at the different kinds of power and how Swift uses her influence to stand up for artists' rights and challenge industry norms. Chapters like "Speak Now"[6] and "The Story of Us"[7] emphasized the importance of building strong relationships and effective teamwork, using Swift's collaborative style as a guide.

"Out of the Woods"[8] discussed crisis management and staying positive during tough times, using Swift's strategic moves, like re-recording her albums, as examples. "Anti-Hero"[9] gave a critical view of idolizing leaders and celebrities, reminding us to approach leadership with context and integrity.

Now, we move from reflection to action. By taking these key lessons from Swift's career, we offer a guide for aspiring leaders who want to inspire, innovate, and lead with integrity. Embrace the principles of having a clear vision, motivating others, being genuine, and staying resilient. Use these strategies in your own leadership journey, adapting them to your unique situation and challenges.

DEFINE YOUR VISION AND SET YOUR GOALS

Taylor Swift's career exemplifies the importance of having a clear vision and setting concrete goals. From a young age, Swift had a clear goal of becoming a successful recording artist in Nashville, which guided her actions and

---

[2]Swift, T. (2023). Sparks Fly [Song]. *On Speak Now* (Taylor's Version). Republic Records.
[3]Swift, T. (2021). Fearless [Song]. *On Fearless* (Taylor's Version). Republic Records.
[4]Swift, T. (2023). Sparks Fly [Song]. *On Speak Now* (Taylor's Version). Republic Records.
[5]Swift, T. (2023). Enchanted [Song]. *On Speak Now* (Taylor's Version). Republic Records.
[6]Swift, T. (2023). Speak Now [Song]. *On Speak Now* (Taylor's Version). Republic Records.
[7]Swift, T. (2023). The Story of Us [Song]. *On Speak Now* (Taylor's Version). Republic Records.
[8]Swift, T. (2021). Out of the Woods [Song]. *On 1989* (Taylor's Version). Republic Records.
[9]Swift, T. (2022). Anti-Hero [Song]. On *Midnights*. Republic Records.

decisions. Her ability to set and pursue challenging yet attainable goals, and to seek and utilize feedback, highlights effective goal-setting practices that can lead to high performance.

> *"I love having a goal, feeling like I'm on a mission. I love trying to beat what I've done so far." – Taylor Swift, Interview with Marie Claire Magazine* (Cutter, 2010)

Action steps:

- *Set clear goals*: Define your vision and break it down into specific, measurable, attainable, relevant, and time-bound (SMART) goals (Doran, 1981). Clearly outline what you want to achieve and establish a timeline for reaching these objectives. Regularly revisit and adjust your goals as needed to stay aligned with your vision.

- *Seek feedback*: Actively seek feedback from mentors, colleagues, and team members to ensure you are on the right track. Constructive criticism can provide valuable insights and help refine your goals. Establish regular check-ins or review sessions to gather and implement feedback effectively.

Allowing yourself to dream and set goals for your future provides a clear sense of direction and purpose, transforming abstract aspirations into concrete plans that guide your daily actions. This process fosters motivation, resilience, and a growth mindset, as you visualize your desired outcomes and chart the steps needed to achieve them. Moreover, engaging others in your goal-setting journey can significantly accelerate your progress. By sharing your dreams and objectives with mentors, colleagues, and supportive peers, you gain access to a wealth of knowledge, experience, and resources that can help overcome obstacles and provide new perspectives. Collaboration fosters accountability, encouragement, and the collective effort necessary to turn ambitious goals into reality, making the path to success both more manageable and enriching (Gordon, 2020).

EMBODYING TRANSFORMATIONAL LEADERSHIP

Swift embodies transformational leadership by inspiring and motivating her fans and followers. She communicates a compelling vision through her music and public appearances, fostering a strong sense of purpose. Her personal story and public speeches emphasize resilience, authenticity, and the importance of learning from failures, which align with the principles of transformational leadership.

> *"I live for the feeling of standing on a stage and saying, 'I feel this way,' and the crowd responding with 'We do too!' And me being like, 'Really?' And they're like, 'Yes!'"* – Taylor Swift, Variety interview (Willman, 2020).

Action steps:

- *Inspire with a vision*: Clearly articulate your vision and share it with your team in a way that is compelling and motivating. Create a sense of purpose that resonates with your team members and aligns with their values and goals. Use storytelling and real-life examples to make your vision more relatable.

- *Lead by example*: Demonstrate resilience and authenticity in your leadership style. Be transparent about your challenges and how you overcame them. Share stories of learning from failures to illustrate that setbacks are opportunities for growth. Your actions will inspire and motivate your team to persevere and strive for excellence.

To be a transformational leader, focus on inspiring and motivating your team by clearly articulating a compelling vision that aligns with their values and goals. Incorporate storytelling as a powerful tool to convey your vision and connect with your team on an emotional level. Transformational leaders foster an environment of trust and enthusiasm, encouraging innovation and creativity. Emphasize the importance of personal development by providing opportunities for learning and growth, and by setting an example of continuous self-improvement. Taylor Swift exemplifies this approach, using her music and public narratives to inspire and engage her audience. Transformational leaders use charisma, inspirational motivation, intellectual stimulation, and individualized consideration to achieve exceptional results (Bass & Riggio, 2006). By challenging the status quo and promoting a culture of open communication and collaboration, and leveraging storytelling to make your vision resonate, you can empower your team to reach their full potential and drive organizational success (Northouse, 2018).

TAP INTO CREATIVITY AND INNOVATION

Swift's approach to her music and business ventures demonstrates the value of creativity and innovation. She continually reinvents her image and sound, taking risks and exploring new opportunities. This willingness to innovate is crucial for leaders who aim to drive progress and encourage creative thinking within their teams.

> *"Creativity is getting inspiration and having that lightning bolt idea moment, and then having the hard work ethic to sit down at the desk and write it down."* – Taylor Swift, Vogue interview (Sabia, 2016).

Action steps:

- *Encourage creative thinking*: Foster an environment where creativity is valued. Organize brainstorming sessions, innovation workshops, and collaborative projects to encourage team members to think outside the box. Create a safe space where ideas can be freely shared and explored without fear of criticism.

- *Embrace risk*: Don't be afraid to take calculated risks. Encourage your team to experiment with new ideas and approaches. Reward innovation and learn from both successes and failures. Recognize that some risks may not pay off immediately, but they can lead to significant breakthroughs in the long run.

As an aspiring leader, prioritizing creativity and innovation within your team is crucial for driving sustained success and adaptability in a rapidly changing world. Embrace the power of creativity to generate novel ideas and solutions, essential for keeping a competitive edge. Cultivate an environment where your team feels free to explore and experiment, leading to breakthrough innovations. Creativity flourishes in settings that support autonomy, provide ample resources, and offer challenging work (Amabile & Pratt, 2016). Moreover, leaders who actively encourage creative thinking and recognize innovative efforts see enhanced team performance and satisfaction (Shalley & Gilson, 2017). By nurturing a culture that values creativity, you not only fuel innovation but also boost morale and engagement, setting the stage for long-term success in your organization.

FOSTER POSITIVE PSYCHOLOGICAL CAPITAL
AND LEARN HOW TO TURN CRISIS INTO OPPORTUNITY

The book explores how Swift handled the crisis of losing control over her master recordings. Her strategic decision to re-record her albums turned a challenging situation into an opportunity for growth and empowerment. This example illustrates the importance of being proactive, maintaining transparency, and cultivating positive psychological capital to enhance resilience and effectively manage crises.

> *"There might be times when you put your whole heart and soul into something, and you're met with cynicism or skepticism, but you can't let that crush you. You have to let that fuel you…"* – Taylor Swift, 2021 Brit Awards speech (Chan, 2021).

Action steps:

- *Proactive strategies*: Develop proactive strategies for potential crises. Identify possible risks and create contingency plans to address them. Regularly review and update these plans to ensure they remain relevant and effective. Encourage your team to stay prepared and adaptable.

- *Transparency*: Communicate openly with your team during crises. Transparency builds trust and fosters a collaborative approach to problem-solving. Keep your team informed about the situation, the steps being taken to address it, and the expected outcomes. This will help maintain morale and encourage collective efforts to overcome challenges.

In times of crisis, your ability to manage effectively and foster positive psychological capital within your team is crucial. First, prioritize transparent communication to build trust and maintain morale; let your team know the facts and what steps are being taken to navigate the crisis. Developing resilience, optimism, hope, and self-efficacy within your team can significantly enhance their ability to cope with challenges. Encourage a growth mindset, where setbacks are viewed as opportunities for learning and development. Additionally, maintaining a supportive environment where team members feel valued and understood can strengthen their commitment and engagement, even under stress (Avey et al., 2011). By cultivating these qualities, you not only guide your team through crises more effectively but also build a more resilient and adaptable workforce for the future.

BE AN ETHICAL AND AUTHENTIC LEADER

Swift's consistent pursuit of authenticity and ethical behavior makes her a role model for ethical leadership. She has been transparent about her struggles and successes, encouraging others to embrace their true selves and act with integrity. Her actions, such as re-recording her albums to regain control over her work, reflect a commitment to ethical principles and personal values.

> *Obviously, anytime you're standing up against or for anything, you're never going to receive unanimous praise. But that's what forces you to be brave. And that's what's different about the way I live my life now.* – Taylor Swift, Variety interview (Willman, 2020).

Action steps:

- *Stay true to your values*: Make decisions that reflect your core values and ethical principles. Consistently act with integrity and fairness, even when it is challenging. This will build trust and respect among your team and stakeholders.

- *Be authentic*: Share your journey, including struggles and successes, with your team. Authenticity fosters trust and loyalty. Be honest about your experiences and encourage others to do the same. This openness creates a supportive environment where everyone feels valued and understood.

Being authentic and ethical as a leader is essential for building trust and respect among your team and stakeholders. Embrace the power of authenticity by staying true to your values and demonstrating integrity in all your actions. Taylor Swift once said, *"Just be yourself, there is no one better"* (Davis, 2023). This principle is crucial in leadership because people are more likely to follow and respect leaders who are genuine and transparent. Additionally, when leaders promote ethical behavior through their actions and relationships, it increases organizational trust and reduces employee turnover (Brown & Treviño, 2006). By embodying these qualities, you can inspire your team and create a positive, trustworthy environment that fosters loyalty and long-term success.

MANAGE A SUCCESSFUL TEAM
AS A SERVANT LEADER

Swift's interactions with her team and fans highlight elements of servant leadership. She prioritizes the needs of her team, provides support and recognition, and fosters a culture of inclusion and empowerment. Aspiring leaders can learn from Swift's methods to build and manage high-performing teams by emphasizing collaboration and mutual respect.

> *No matter what happens in life, be good to people. Being good to people is a wonderful legacy to leave behind.* – Taylor Swift (Haden, 2023).

Action steps:

- *Prioritize team needs*: Put the needs of your team first. Focus on providing the support and resources they need to succeed. Regularly check in with team members to understand their challenges and help them overcome obstacles.

- *Foster inclusion*: Create an inclusive environment where everyone feels valued and respected. Encourage diverse perspectives and collaboration. Recognize and celebrate the unique contributions of each team member. This approach will build a cohesive and high-performing team.

To effectively manage your team as a servant leader, prioritize the needs and well-being of your team members. Foster a supportive and inclusive environment that empowers each individual to perform at their best. Focus on serving rather than commanding; emphasize empathy, active listening, and the personal and professional growth of your team members. This leadership style has been shown to enhance team performance, satisfaction, and cohesion by creating a culture of trust and collaboration (Greenleaf, 1977). Research indicates that servant leadership leads to higher levels of employee engagement and commitment, as employees feel valued and supported in their roles (Liden et al., 2008). By investing in the development of your team and prioritizing their needs, you can inspire loyalty, drive innovation, and achieve sustainable success.

LEARN HOW TO EFFECTIVELY COMMUNICATE AND POSITIVELY INFLUENCE OTHERS

Effective communication is a hallmark of Swift's leadership style. She knows how to connect with her audience, using her platform to convey meaningful messages and inspire action. Leaders can draw valuable lessons from her ability to communicate with confidence, tailor messages to different audiences, and use storytelling as a powerful tool for influence.

> *"Communication is really important because I want people to know how they're making me feel and why I'm doing what I'm doing."*
> – Taylor Swift, Rolling Stone interview (Eells, 2014).

Action steps:

- *Use storytelling*: Incorporate storytelling into your communication strategy. Share personal anecdotes, case studies, and success stories to make your messages more engaging and relatable. Storytelling can help convey complex ideas in a simple and memorable way.

- *Tailor messages*: Adapt your communication style to suit different audiences. Ensure that your messages are clear, compelling, and resonate with your listeners. Consider the needs and perspectives of your audience when crafting your messages to maximize their impact.

As an aspiring leader, communicating with confidence and tailoring your messages to different audiences is crucial for effective leadership. Confidence in communication helps convey authority and earn respect, while adapting your message ensures it resonates with diverse groups. Research shows that leaders who communicate confidently and clearly are more likely to inspire and motivate their teams (Cuddy et al., 2013). Additionally, using storytelling as a tool can significantly enhance your influence. Stories create an emotional connection, making your message more memorable and impactful. According to Denning (2005), storytelling is a powerful tool for leaders as it helps convey complex ideas, values, and visions in a relatable and engaging manner.

BE ADAPTABLE

Taylor Swift's career demonstrates the importance of adaptability in the face of change and adversity. She has continuously evolved her music and public persona to stay relevant and impactful. Leaders must balance adaptability with steadfastness in their values to navigate complex and changing environments effectively.

> *"Part of growing up and moving into new chapters of your life is about catch and release. What I mean by that is, knowing what things to keep, and what things to release."* – Taylor Swift, 2022 NYU Commencement Speech (Dailey, 2022).

Action steps:

- *Embrace change*: Be open to change and willing to adapt your strategies. Stay informed about industry trends and emerging challenges. Encourage your team to embrace change and view it as an opportunity for growth and innovation.

- *Foster a culture of flexibility*: Promote a workplace culture where flexibility is valued. Encourage team members to experiment with new approaches and support them in pivoting when necessary. Provide resources and training that enhance adaptability skills.

Adaptability is key to effectively navigating the ever-changing landscape of business. Being adaptable means being open to new ideas, willing to change strategies when necessary, and staying resilient in the face of challenges. Leaders who demonstrate adaptability are better equipped to manage uncertainty and drive organizational success (Yukl & Mahsud, 2010). Furthermore, adaptability is linked to improved decision-making and problem-solving, as flexible leaders can adjust their approach based on situational demands (Pulakos et al., 2000). Embracing adaptability not only helps you respond to changes but also fosters innovation and growth within your team, making you a more effective and dynamic leader.

LEARN FROM FAILURE

Swift openly discusses her failures and setbacks, framing them as essential learning experiences. This perspective encourages a growth mindset and resilience, essential traits for leaders who aim to continuously improve and lead by example.

> *"I've come to a realization that I need to be able to forgive myself for making the wrong choice, trusting the wrong person, or figuratively falling on my face in front of everyone. Step into the daylight and let it go."* – Taylor Swift, Elle Magazine (Swift, 2019).

Action steps:

- *Encourage a growth mindset*: Promote a culture where failures are viewed as opportunities for growth. Encourage your team to take risks, learn from mistakes, and continuously strive for improvement. Provide constructive feedback and support to help them grow.

- *Build resilience*: Cultivate resilience by maintaining a positive outlook and learning from setbacks. Provide support and resources to help your team build resilience. Encourage a culture of continuous improvement and learning, where failures are seen as valuable lessons rather than setbacks.

Learning from failure and maintaining a growth mindset are critical components of personal and professional development. Embracing a growth mindset means viewing challenges and setbacks not as insurmountable obstacles but as valuable opportunities for learning and improvement. This perspective encourages resilience and adaptability, enabling you to persevere through difficulties and emerge stronger. Research by Dweck (2006) highlights that people with a growth mindset are more likely to embrace challenges and persist in the face of setbacks. Moreover, by analyzing and understanding the reasons behind failures, we can implement effective strategies to avoid similar pitfalls in the future, fostering continuous growth and innovation. Adopting this approach not only enhances your personal growth but also cultivates a culture of continuous improvement within the teams and organizations (Smith, 2018) that you are a part of.

APPRECIATE AND RESPECT DIVERSITY

Swift's inclusive approach and respect for diversity are evident in her interactions with fans and collaborators. She acknowledges and celebrates differences, creating a welcoming and supportive environment. Leaders can learn from her example to foster diversity and inclusion within their teams and organizations.

> *"In 10 years I've seen forward steps in our industry, in our aware-ness, our inclusion, our ability to start calling out unfairness and misconduct."* – Taylor Swift, Billboard's Woman of the Decade acceptance speech (Schiller, 2019).

Action steps:

- *Promote inclusivity*: Implement policies and practices that promote diversity and inclusion. Provide training and resources to educate your team on the importance of respecting differences and creating an inclu-sive workplace. Regularly review and update these policies to ensure they remain effective.

- *Celebrate differences*: Acknowledge and celebrate the diverse back-grounds and perspectives of your team members. Create opportunities for team members to share their experiences and learn from each other. This will foster a culture of mutual respect and understanding.

Promoting diversity and inclusion within your organization will be key to your success as a leader. Actively fostering an inclusive culture ensures that all employees feel valued and respected, which, in turn, enhances the organiza-tion's performance and creativity. Diverse teams bring a variety of perspec-tives and ideas, leading to better problem-solving and decision-making (Page, 2007). Additionally, inclusive practices are linked to higher employee engage-ment and retention, as people are more likely to stay with a company where they feel accepted and appreciated (Roberson, 2006). By championing diver-sity and inclusion, you can build a stronger, more cohesive, and successful organization, positioning yourself as an effective and forward-thinking leader.

CONCLUSION

Taylor Swift's journey shows the power of visionary and authentic leader-ship. She inspires through her music, connects personally with her audience, and navigates the music industry's complexities, offering valuable lessons for future leaders. Embracing transformational leadership, promoting creativity and innovation, and committing to diversity and inclusion can lead to lasting success.

This book has explored Swift's strategic decision-making, resilience, ethical behavior, and continuous growth. By applying these lessons, you can develop a leadership style that achieves great results and inspires those around you. Taylor Swift demonstrates that effective leadership requires ongoing self-improvement, adaptability, and the courage to be true to oneself.

REFERENCES

Amabile, T. M., & Pratt, M. G. (2016). The dynamic componential model of creativity and innovation in organizations: Making progress, making meaning. *Research in Organizational Behavior, 36*, 157–183.

Avey, J. B., Reichard, R. J., Luthans, F., & Mhatre, K. H. (2011). Meta-analysis of the impact of positive psychological capital on employee attitudes, behaviors, and performance. *Human Resource Development Quarterly, 22*(2), 127–152.

Bass, B. M., & Riggio, R. E. (2006). *Transformational leadership*. Psychology Press.

Brown, M. E., & Treviño, L. K. (2006). Ethical leadership: A review and future directions. *The Leadership Quarterly, 17*(6), 595–616.

Chan, A. (2021, April 18). Taylor Swift offers inspiration in Brit awards 2021 speech: "you have the right to prove them wrong." *Billboard*. https://www.billboard.com/music/awards/taylor-swift-inspires-with-brit-awards-2021-speech-video-9570789/

Cuddy, A. J., Kohut, M., & Neffinger, J. (2013). Connect, then lead. *Harvard Business Review, 91*(7/8), 54–61.

Cutter, K. (2010, June 2). Taylor Swift's rise to America's sweetheart. *Marie Claire Magazine*. https://www.marieclaire.com/celebrity/a4828/taylor-swift-interview-quotes/

Dailey, H. (2022, May 18). Taylor Swift's NYU Commencement speech: Read the full transcript. *Billboard*. https://www.billboard.com/music/music-news/taylor-swift-nyu-commencement-speech-full-transcript-1235072824/

Davis, H. (2023, July 19). *27 awesome Taylor Swift quotes to live your life by*. Music In Minnesota. https://www.musicinminnesota.com/taylor-swift-quotes/

Denning, S. (2005). *The leader's guide to storytelling: Mastering the art and discipline of business narrative*. Jossey-Bass.

Doran, G. T. (1981). There's a S.M.A.R.T. way to write management's goals and objectives. *Management Review, 70*(11), 35–36.

Dweck, C. S. (2006). *Mindset: The new psychology of success*. Random House.

Eells, J. (2014, April 19). *Cover story: The reinvention of Taylor Swift*. Rolling Stone. https://www.rollingstone.com/music/music-news/the-reinvention-of-taylor-swift-116925/

Gordon, J. (2020). The power of collaboration in achieving goals. *Journal of Organizational Behavior, 35*(4), 567–580.

Greenleaf, R. K. (1977). *Servant leadership: A journey into the nature of legitimate power and greatness*. Paulist Press.

Haden, J. (2023). Taylor Swift says living a happy, successful, and meaningful life comes down to 5 things. *Inc.com*. https://www.inc.com/jeff-haden/taylor-swift-says-living-a-happy-successful-meaningful-life-comes-down-to-5-simple-things.html

Liden, R. C., Wayne, S. J., Zhao, H., & Henderson, D. (2008). Servant leadership: Development of a multidimensional measure and multi-level assessment. *The Leadership Quarterly, 19*(2), 161–177.

Northouse, P. G. (2018). *Leadership: Theory and practice* (8th ed.). Sage Publications.

Page, S. E. (2007). *The difference: How the power of diversity creates better groups, firms, schools, and societies*. Princeton University Press.

Pulakos, E. D., Arad, S., Donovan, M. A., & Plamondon, K. E. (2000). Adaptability in the workplace: Development of a taxonomy of adaptive performance. *Journal of Applied Psychology, 85*(4), 612.

Roberson, Q. M. (2006). Disentangling the meanings of diversity and inclusion in organizations. *Group & Organization Management, 31*(2), 212–236.

Sabia, J. (2016, April 19). *73 questions with Taylor Swift | vogue*. YouTube. https://www.youtube.com/watch?v=XnbCSboujF4

Schiller, R. (2019, December 13). Taylor Swift accepts woman of the decade award at Billboard's women in music: Read her full speech. *Billboard*. https://www.billboard.com/music/awards/taylor-swift-woman-of-the-decade-speech-billboard-women-in-music-8546156/

Shalley, C. E., & Gilson, L. L. (2017). Creativity and the management of technology: Balancing creativity and standardization. *Management Science, 63*(3), 548–563.

Smith, R. (2018). The positive power of failure: Using mistakes to enhance performance and growth. *Journal of Business Psychology, 33*(2), 253–264.

Swift, T. (2019). Taylor Swift on 30 things she learned before her 30th birthday – Taylor Swift turns 30. *Elle Magazine*. https://www.elle.com/culture/celebrities/a26628467/taylor-swift-30th-birthday-lessons/

Willman, C. (2020, January 21). Taylor Swift: No longer "polite at all costs." *Variety*. https://variety.com/2020/music/features/taylor-swift-politics-sundance-documentary-miss-americana-1203471910/

Yukl, G., & Mahsud, R. (2010). Why flexible and adaptive leadership is essential. *Consulting Psychology Journal: Practice and Research, 62*(2), 81.

INDEX

Adaptability, 102
Adversity, 72
All Too Well (song), 93
    adaptable, 102
    appreciate and respect diversity,
        103–104
    embodying transformational
        leadership, 95–97
    ethical and authentic leader, 99
    foster positive psychological capital
        and learn to turn crisis into
        opportunity, 98
    learn from failure, 102
    learn to effectively communicate and
        positively influence, 101
    manage successful team as servant
        leader, 100
    tap into creativity and innovation, 97
    vision and set goals, 94–95
Anti-hero, 86, 94
    hero worship, 86–88
    potential missteps in Swift's
        Leadership, 88–90
Apple Music, 23
Appreciation for fans, 30
Artistic goals, 65
Artistic integrity, 30
Aspiration, 12
Authentic leaders, 20, 30, 99
Authentic leadership style, 28, 30–31
Authenticity, 20, 96
Authority, 38

Bases of power, 38
Big Machine Label Group (BMLG), 76
Big Machine Records, 32, 74
Billboard, 19
Bonding social capital, 60–61

Brand, 72
Bridging social capital, 60, 62
Business, 49, 62
    goals, 65
    leadership, 57
    model, 39

Career decisions, 63
Casual listeners, 52
Celebrities, 86
    problems from emulating, 87–88
Charisma, 43
Charismatic leaders, 44
Citizenship behaviours, 14
Close-knit circle, 64
Coercion, 38
Communication, 50
Communication plans, 74
Comprehensive framework, 64
Conceptual framework, 72
Confidence, 101
Constructive criticism, 95
Counterproductive behaviors, 14
COVID-19 pandemic, 52
Creativity, 28–29
    tap into creativity and innovation, 97
Crisis into opportunity, foster positive
        psychological capital and learn
        to turn, 98
Crisis management, 5, 72
    damage containment, 74
    five phases of, 72
    learning, 75–77
    plans, 74
    preparation/prevention, 74
    recovery, 74–75
    signal detection, 73–74
    strategies, 76

Criticisms, 88
Critics, 86
Cultures, 88
Customer feedback, 73

Data breach, 75
Decision-maker, 2
Decision-making process, 5, 7, 21, 50,
        102, 104
Decisions, 2
Democratic process, 55
Diverse teams, 104
Dreams, 13

"Easter egg hunt", 21
Effective communication, 101
Effective leaders, 78
Effective teamwork, 94
Efficacy, 78
Embrace risk, 97
Emotional investment, 65
Employees, 23
Empowering leadership, 50
"Enchanted" (Song), 4, 37, 94
Encourage creative thinking, 97
Encourage team members, 102
Energetic bursts, 27
Energy, 43
Entrepreneurial leadership style, 28, 32
Entrepreneurial opportunity, 33
Eras Tour, 6, 31, 33
Ethical behaviours, 20
Ethical leader, 99
Evermore (albums), 80
Expert power, 42–43
Extensive networks, 62
External stakeholder, 74

Fans, 22–23, 32
    kindness and appreciation for fans,
        30
Fashion, 62
Fearless, 17, 94
    idealized influence, 20
    individualized consideration, 22–23
    inspirational motivation, 19
    intellectual stimulation, 21
    transformational leadership, 18–19
Financial institution, 75
Financial interests, 72
Flexible leaders, 102

Folklore, 80
Forbes, 20
Foster positive psychological capital
        and learn to turn crisis into
        opportunity, 98
Fostering connections, 41

Genuine enthusiasm and effort, 19
Goals, 13, 18, 87
    attainment, 12, 14
    goal-setting practices, 95
    goal–setting theory, 3, 12–13
Groundbreaking achievements, 43
Growth mindset, 103

Hackman's five factors of team
        effectiveness, 64–66
Hackman's team effectiveness model, 59
Hands-on approach, 65
Hard work, 31
Haters, 52
Hero worship, 86
    potential dangers of, 86
    problems from emulating celebrities,
        87–88
Heroes, 86
High–performing team, 60
Hope, 77–78

Idealized influence, 18, 20
Individualized consideration, 18, 22–23
Influencer, 2
Innovation, 28–29
    tap into creativity and, 97
Innovative ideas, 27
Inspiration, 27
Inspirational motivation, 18–19
Intellectual stimulation, 18, 21
Internal stakeholder, 74
International multimedia superstars, 2

Job
    performance, 14
    satisfaction, 50

Kindness for fans, 30
Knowledge workers, 42

Leader's in-group, 50
Leader–Member Exchange Theory
        (LMX Theory), 4, 50–53

Leaders, 102, 104
Leadership, 3, 49
  styles and behaviors, 29
  theories, 50
Learning, 75
  phase, 75
Legitimate power, 41–42
LGBTQ+ community, 55
Life-changing, 7
Los Angeles Times (Newspaper), 63
Lover album, 76

Magical allure, 37
Media, 62
Mega Mentor, 66
Meta-analysis of leadership, 28
Midnights (album), 65, 80
Music, 62
  industry, 41, 43, 55–56, 93
  label, 32
  streaming service, 39
Musical collaborations, 63
Musical impact, 41
Musical prodigy, 15

Nashville, vision of, 13–14
Natural disaster, 75
Natural talent, 87
Nature of power, 37
New York Times, 63
New York University (NYU), 19
New Yorker, The (Magazine), 31

One-on-one relationships, 50
Opportunities, 96, 104
  foster positive psychological capital
    and learn to turn crisis into, 98
Optimism, 79–80
Optimistic leaders, 79
Organizational behavior, 77
Organizational citizenship behaviours,
    51
Organizational crisis, 72
Organizational goals, 32
Organizational learning, 73
Organizations, 20
Out of the Woods (Song), 4, 72, 94
  five phases of crisis management,
    72–77
  positive psychological capital, 77–80

Out-groups, 51
Own leadership, 90

Performer, 43
Personal development, 30, 96
Personal goals, 14
Personal growth, 100
Personal power, 43
Personalized approach, 52
Political power, 42
Popular culture, 2
Positive emotions, 86
Positive psychological capital, 72,
    77, 98
  efficacy, 78
  hope, 77–78
  optimism, 79–80
  resilience, 78
Power, 38–44
  coercive power, 38–39
  expert power, 42–43
  legitimate power, 41–42
  referent power, 43–44
  reward power, 39–41
Praise, 41
Proactive crisis management, 75
Proactive strategies, 98
Problem-solving, 102, 104
Professional growth, 100
Promotion, 39
Psychological capital (PsyCap), 77
Psychology, 77

Re-release process, 32
Recognition, 41
Recovery, 74–75
Referent power, 43–44
Relationships, 50
Resilience, 19, 31, 78, 96
Reward power, 39–41
Risk assessments, 74
Role models, 20, 44, 86
Royalty payments, 39

Secret sessions, 51
Seek feedback, 95
Self-awareness, 30
Self-efficacy, 78–79
Self-leadership, 13
Sentiment, 42

Servant leader, manage successful team
     as, 100
Servant leadership, 53–56, 100
Sexual assault, 55
Signal detection, 73–74
Singer, 43–44
Social capital model, 59
Social capital theory, 60–64
Social group, 88
Social influence, 38
Social media, 39, 44, 51, 53, 73
Social networks, 60
Social relationships, 60
Social skills, 43
Songwriter, 43–44
Sparks Fly, 27, 94
     authentic leadership style, 30–31
     creativity and innovation, 28–29
     entrepreneurial leadership, 32
     leadership styles and behaviors, 29
Speak Now (Song), 27, 94
     leader–member exchange theory,
          50–53
     servant leadership, 53–56
Speaking events, 19
Specific, measurable, attainable,
          relevant, and time-bound goals
          (SMART goals), 95
Spotify, 39
     two-tier customer business model, 39
Story of Us, The, 94
     Hackman's five factors of team
          effectiveness, 64–66
     social capital theory, 60–64
Storytelling, 101
Strategic relationships, 60
Supervisors, 39
Supportive environment, 18, 29, 66, 99
Swift, T., 1, 11, 18–19, 21–22, 40
     approach, 5
     dream, 11
     Eras tour, 6
     focus on, 5–7
     influences, 88
     leadership, 18, 85, 94
     optimism, resilience, and
          confidence, 72

own leadership approach, 2
potential missteps in swift's
     leadership, 88–90
proactive approach, 72
songs, 89
vision, 11
willingness, 23
Swifties, 4, 31–32, 51, 53

Task behaviours, 14–15
Task performance, 14–15
Taylor's Versions, 80
Team effectiveness, Hackman's five
     factors of, 64–66
TennesSee Equality Project
     (TEP), 55
Tortured Poets Department,
     The, 89
Traditional leadership, 53–54
Transformational leaders, 21, 96
Transformational leadership, 18–19, 94
     embodying, 95–97
Transparency, 98
Two-way communication, 22

Valuable resource, 40
Value systems, 42
Vision, 18, 43, 96
     of nashville, 13–14
     and set goals, 94–95
Visionary leadership, 3, 12
Visual boundaries, 19
Voice, The, 66
Voter registration, 55

"Walking the walk", 20
Walt Disney, 15
Wild dream, 11
"Wildest Dreams", 11, 94
     goal-setting theory, 12–13
     task behaviors and task performance,
          14–15
     vision of Nashville, 13–14
     visionary leadership, 12
Work ethic, 15
Workplace innovation, 28
Worst case scenario

www.ingramcontent.com/pod-product-compliance
Lightning Source LLC
Chambersburg PA
CBHW061258220326
41599CB00028B/5701